LOW-SODIUM
MEAL PREP
COOKBOOK

LOW-SODIUM MEAL PREP COOKBOOK

6 Weeks of Easy, Flavorful Make-Ahead Meals

Ayla Shaw, RDN, MS

ROCKRIDGE
PRESS

For general information on our other products and services or to obtain technical support, please contact our Customer Care Department within the United States at (866) 744-2665, or outside the United States at (510) 253-0500.

Rockridge Press publishes its books in a variety of electronic and print formats. Some content that appears in print may not be available in electronic books, and vice versa.

TRADEMARKS: Rockridge Press and the Rockridge Press logo are trademarks or registered trademarks of Callisto Media Inc. and/or its affiliates, in the United States and other countries, and may not be used without written permission. All other trademarks are the property of their respective owners. Rockridge Press is not associated with any product or vendor mentioned in this book.

Interior and Cover Designer: Carlos Esparza
Art Producer: Megan Baggott
Editor: Anne Goldberg
Production Editor: Jenna Dutton
Production Manager: Holly Haydash

Cover photo, ii, 88 ©2021 Hélène Dujardin. Food styling by Anna Hampton.

Darren Muir, vi, 38; Marija Vidal, viii; Cody & Nat Ganz, x; Profimedia/StockFood USA, 22; Susan Brooks-Dammann/StockFood USA, 56; Cameron Whitman/Stocksy, 72; Nadine Greeff, 103; Amanda Stockley/StockFood USA, 104; Elysa Weitala, 117

Author photo courtesy of Kaylin Perkins

Paperback ISBN: 978-1-63807-041-2
eBook ISBN: 978-1-63807-291-1

R0

For Scout and all my patients who inspired me through their journeys to write this book and use their experiences to help others.

CONTENTS

INTRODUCTION

Welcome to your low-sodium meal prep guide. I am honored you chose my book to take you on this journey. I designed this meal prep plan to be as straightforward as possible for easy-to-cook, flavorful meals. Don't worry; you don't need to be a gourmet chef to follow these recipes!

Everyone who knew me growing up was shocked when I announced my career change to dietitian. I was a picky eater while living in the suburbs of Atlanta, where I got my undergraduate degree in statistics from the University of Georgia. After graduating, I moved to the city of Atlanta and worked for a commercial insurance company doing catastrophe modeling.

I began to explore my relationship with food and expand my abilities in the kitchen in my early twenties. As my relationship with food blossomed, I witnessed several family members struggle with chronic illnesses, such as type 1 diabetes and cancer. I saw how diet played a crucial role in treating these conditions. These experiences inspired me to go back to school, and I completed my master's degree in health science with a concentration in nutrition from Georgia State University. After a yearlong dietetic internship at Yale New Haven Hospital, I passed my board exams to become a registered dietitian nutritionist.

For the next few years, I worked in a hospital and delivered low-sodium diet education with individuals who had experienced major health events like a stroke or heart attack. Eventually, I started working in outpatient counseling because I felt it was more effective to work with patients if I could get to them *before* they had significant health issues. Since starting my nutrition practice, hundreds of individuals have come to me for a low-sodium diet.

Far too often, my clients complain about how their days get away from them with little to no time to cook, so they turn to convenience foods—i.e., salt-filled food

that requires little to no preparation. While their underlying diagnoses vary, their struggles with salt are similar. This is why meal prep is so beneficial to individuals struggling with following a low-sodium diet. By setting aside a few hours one day a week, all meals are prepared and ready to grab and go for the week, eliminating the need for high-sodium convenience foods.

Another common scenario in my office is the patient who lets the fear of sacrificing flavor trump the fear of their health concern. Feeling their food will be bland, these patients are hesitant to cook without salt, not realizing the amount of sodium in their food. You don't have to live your life eating boring food with no taste to follow a low-sodium diet. I created this book to show you how to add tons of flavor to food without using salt. It may take some time for your taste buds to adjust, so be patient with yourself.

My clients who have successfully reduced their sodium intake have seen many positive health benefits as a result. Benefits can range from a decrease in medication to eliminating the need for blood pressure medicine at all! A 2017 study published in the *Journal of the American College of Cardiology* found a low-sodium diet was as effective at controlling high blood pressure as antihypertensive drugs. Many of my clients find meal prep to be helpful with weight loss and diabetes management as well.

Even if you haven't developed any serious medical conditions, following this meal prep guide will provide you with a well-balanced plan to improve your overall health and prevent illness in the future. Whatever your motivation for picking it up, I hope this book provides you with guidance on preparing delicious low-sodium meals for yourself and starts you on your journey to better health.

CHAPTER ONE

Meal Prep and a Low-Sodium Diet

Before we get to the delicious recipes, we must cover some of the basics. You may be tempted to skip past this chapter, but I encourage you to keep reading. The fundamentals discussed here are the building blocks for your long-term success.

It's like the old saying: "Give a man a fish, and you feed him for a day. Teach a man to fish, and you feed him for his life." Simply following the weekly meal prep plans in this book will help reduce your sodium intake, but without knowing the principles behind them, you'd have to repeat the six weeks of meal plans to maintain the diet. Alternatively, you can really dive into the content of this book and learn how to plan and prepare low-sodium meals for yourself.

The Positive Side of Sodium

Sodium is a naturally occurring mineral that is necessary for our bodies to function. It is mostly found in our diets in the form of salt, or sodium chloride. As with other vitamins and minerals, the body obtains sodium through our diet, so you must consume enough of it—but not too much! For our purposes, this book uses "sodium" and "salt" interchangeably. Some of sodium's most important functions include:

- **FLUID BALANCE.** Sodium, along with other minerals we call "electrolytes," is necessary for keeping the balance of fluid between the inside and outside of our cells. Too much sodium can cause fluid retention and swelling, most notably in the extremities.

- **MUSCLE CONTRACTION.** Electrolytes create nerve impulses and are essential for our muscles to contract properly. Ever had a muscle cramp while exercising? This is often from electrolyte imbalance caused by drinking water to rehydrate but not replacing electrolytes—like sodium—that we lose in sweat.

- **BLOOD VOLUME.** Sodium is directly related to the amount of blood in your body. High amounts of sodium increase the amount of blood in the body. Too much blood in your body can cause high blood pressure. If sodium concentrations are too low, your blood volume decreases, making it harder for your heart to pump it to all your organs.

Insufficient sodium can result in symptoms ranging from headache, nausea, and muscle cramps to seizures and coma in the most severe cases.

The Negative Impacts of Sodium

You go to your annual doctor's visit and are diagnosed with a new condition; you had a significant health scare or maybe you just want to prevent one from happening. There are many reasons your doctor may instruct you to follow a low-sodium diet. Most of the time, the doctor sends you home with a sheet of paper telling you not to eat all the foods you usually enjoy. It can be scary, stressful, and overwhelming trying to navigate this new lifestyle. This need for support brings many clients to my office and is probably why you purchased this book. Here are some of the most common conditions that can be ameliorated with a low-sodium diet.

A Love Affair with Salt

While salt may have been necessary for food preservation before the invention of refrigeration, more than 100 years after the refrigerator became a fixture in homes, the average American still consumes about 1.5 times the recommended sodium limit each day. That's an average of 3,400mg of sodium each day, whereas the USDA recommends a max of 2,300mg per day, and the American Heart Association (AHA) recommends 1,500mg per day.

This overconsumption may be partially due to the prevalence of salt in convenience foods like frozen dinners, canned soups, and fast food. The AHA estimates that 9 out of 10 Americans are overeating sodium from three main sources: processed foods sold in stores contributing 65 percent, food cooked in restaurants providing 25 percent, and foods cooked at home making up 10 percent. Most of us have grown up with so much sodium in our food that it is what we are used to eating.

HYPERTENSION

"Hypertension" is the medical term for high blood pressure. Blood pressure measures the force that your blood exerts on the walls of your blood vessels. Sodium stays inside your blood vessels and attracts water. Sodium levels need to stay at a certain concentration in your blood. When you have extra sodium in your body, it draws excess water into your blood vessels, increasing the pressure inside. Like how a water balloon expands as it fills, the more water inside the balloon, the tighter and thinner the outside gets.

Blood pressure fluctuates throughout the day, and your body has mechanisms to help lower blood pressure when it becomes elevated. Short periods of elevated blood pressure will likely have little effect on your health. However, when blood pressure remains elevated for a significant period, it can start to damage your blood vessels, heart, and kidneys. Think of it like a rubber band that gets stretched out and loses elasticity over time from being pulled tight over and over.

HEART DISEASE

Low-sodium diets are important for the treatment and prevention of all forms of heart disease. When your blood pressure is higher, your heart works harder. Increased strain on the heart can cause damage over time and worsen preexisting coronary conditions. Additionally, a low-sodium diet helps relieve stress on the heart by reducing excess fluid around it and the lungs that can build up due to heart damage or high blood pressure. This fluid puts additional strain on the heart and can cause discomfort and shortness of breath. Reducing sodium in the diet can also alleviate issues with excess fluid in the legs, another common symptom of heart failure.

KIDNEY DISEASE

In addition to the heart, elevated blood pressure makes the kidneys work harder and can damage them, leading to kidney disease. According to the National Institute of Diabetes and Digestive and Kidney Diseases, diabetes and hypertension are the two leading causes of chronic kidney disease (CKD). Although kidney disease can happen for reasons other than hypertension or diabetes, the kidneys are necessary for filtering excess sodium out of the body. When they are damaged, sodium can build up in the blood. Therefore, it is essential to follow a low-sodium diet to prevent further damage no matter what type of kidney disease you have.

LIVER DISEASE

Fluid retention, referred to as edema or ascites, is a common complication of liver disease. This is again due to the role sodium plays in retaining excess water. A low-sodium diet is often recommended as the first intervention to treat or prevent these complications in patients with liver failure. Recommended sodium intake varies per individual depending on the degree of excess fluid.

MÉNIÈRE'S DISEASE

Ménière's disease affects the inner ear and can cause dizzy spells and even lead to hearing loss. The underlying cause of this condition is unknown, but most symptoms have been tied to an abundance of fluid in the ear. Maintaining a low-sodium intake is recommended to help manage symptoms of this disease.

Is Everyone's "Low Sodium" the Same?

The definition of "low sodium" may not be the same for everyone. Target levels for sodium are different depending on your personal medical history. For most individuals without a significant medical history, the USDA recommends a daily sodium limit of 2,300mg—about the quantity in a teaspoon of table salt—to prevent high blood pressure. For individuals with hypertension or kidney or liver disease, or anyone at an elevated risk of developing these conditions, the AHA recommends limiting sodium intake to less than 1,500mg per day. Because everyone's body is different, some individuals may need more or less sodium than indicated in these recommendations. This is why it is important to speak with your doctor or a dietitian if you struggle to determine your appropriate sodium level.

For the purposes of this book, we will not be adding salt to the recipes. Because the recipes in this book all have less than 500mg per serving, daily sodium intake will be less than 1,500mg each day if you follow the meal plans. This means some individuals may be able to add a total of ⅓ to ½ teaspoon of salt to meals each day and still stay below 2,300mg.

Adjusting to a Low-Sodium Diet

Making the change to a low-sodium diet requires some adjustments to your lifestyle, but it doesn't mean you have to give up everything you enjoy and eat sad, boring food with no flavor for the rest of your life. Here are some of the biggest adjustments you can make to reduce sodium in your diet.

SAYING NO TO PROCESSED FOODS

Processed foods are foods altered from their natural state. According to the US Food and Drug Administration (FDA), this includes washing, cleaning, milling, cutting, chopping, heating, pasteurizing, blanching, cooking, canning, freezing, drying, dehydrating, mixing, packaging, or other procedures including the addition of substances deemed to be safe for consumption, such as salt. Salt is often added to processed foods to boost flavor, maintain freshness, or improve texture. Cutting back on processed foods can help reduce your sodium intake.

Processed foods are one of the biggest contributors to sodium in American diets. The amount of processing a food undergoes can vary, ranging from bagged lettuce to cheese puffs. Highly processed foods have undergone numerous alterations, often including the addition of sodium.

Minimally processed foods close to their natural state, like pre-cut or frozen fruits and vegetables (without any sauces or seasoning), generally have little added sodium. When you need to use processed foods, read nutrition labels to choose the lower-sodium ones. Try to choose foods that are as close to their natural state as possible.

COOKING AT HOME

One of the other largest contributors to sodium in American diets is food purchased outside the home. Whether it's fast food or fine dining, restaurants use a lot of salt because it is a cost-effective way to make food taste good. Food and beverage industry insiders believe that salty foods increase both thirst and beverage sales, although I cannot find any scientific evidence to back this up. No matter the reason, we know restaurant food is high in sodium. Some restaurant meals may contain more than the recommended daily limit of sodium in one serving. For example, a Quiznos 12-inch Classic Italian sandwich contains 3,760mg of sodium, according to the company's website.

Cooking at home is the best way to control what's in your food. When you cook, you can easily monitor sodium intake by choosing salt-free and low-sodium ingredients and seasonings. This is another reason meal prep can be helpful for busy individuals struggling to follow a low-sodium diet.

READJUSTING YOUR TASTE BUDS

According to the Centers for Disease Control and Prevention (CDC), salt is an acquired taste, meaning the more salt we add to food, the less we taste it. We end up adding more salt, which overpowers the other flavors in food. However, over time your taste buds adjust to a low-sodium diet. I can't tell you how often patients come to me after cutting back on their sodium to tell me they ate a dish they hadn't had for a while and now it tastes saltier than before. As your taste buds adjust to lower sodium levels, you will begin to appreciate some of the other flavors in food, like acidity, bitterness, spice, and sourness.

Smart Shopping Strategies

Shopping can be stressful when you start a low-sodium diet, especially once you start realizing that most foods have sodium. You're standing in the store asking yourself: What foods should I purchase, and what should I avoid? How much sodium is too much sodium? What do all these labels mean? To help maintain your sanity, this section will answer those questions and outline strategies for shopping for good health.

READ EVERY LABEL

Nutrition labels on food products are notorious for being confusing. Companies use claims on their products to entice you to buy them, but these statements can be misleading. My clients are constantly coming to me with questions about labels, so let's talk about them.

When it comes to sodium, the FDA defines sodium-related labels on products as:

- *Salt-Free* or *Sodium-Free*: Less than 5mg per serving

- *Very Low Sodium*: Less than 35mg per serving

- *Low Sodium*: Less than 140mg per serving

- *Reduced Sodium*: The product contains at least 25 percent less sodium than the original product. **Be careful because reduced-sodium products can still be high in sodium!**

- *Unsalted* or *No Salt Added*: No additional salt has been added to the product during processing. **These products may still be high in sodium.**

Sodium comes in many forms other than salt, and some foods high in sodium may not even taste salty! Sodium bicarbonate, also known as baking soda, is found in sweet baked goods like cakes, muffins, and cookies. Some other terms for sodium you may see on an ingredient label are monosodium glutamate (MSG), disodium phosphate, sodium ascorbate, sodium nitrate, sodium caseinate, sodium propionate, sodium sulfite, and sodium alginate.

The best way to determine how much sodium is in a food is to look at the nutrition facts label. This will tell you the exact number of milligrams of sodium per serving. The serving size is listed at the top of the label. About halfway down you will find the sodium content in milligrams and percent of the recommended daily limit for healthy individuals (2,300mg).

Nutrition Facts

8 servings per container

Serving size 1 cup (68g)

Amount per serving

Calories 370

	% Daily Value*
Total Fat 5g	**7%**
Saturated Fat 1g	**3%**
Trans Fat 0g	
Cholesterol 0mg	**0%**
Sodium 150mg	6%
Total Carbohydrate 48g	**15%**
Dietary Fiber 5g	**14%**
Total Sugars 13g	
Includes 10g Added Sugars	**20%**
Protein 12g	

Vit. D 2mcg 10%	•	Calcium 210mg 20%
Zinc 7mg 50%	•	Biotin 300mcg 100%

* The % Daily Value (DV) tells you how much a nutrient in a serving of food contributes to a daily diet. 2,000 calories a day is used for general nutrition advice.

HIDDEN SOURCES OF SODIUM

Sodium is hidden in many foods you would not expect. Taste is not a reliable indicator of food's sodium content because salt is an acquired taste and sodium can be found in ingredients other than salt. Just because a food doesn't taste salty doesn't mean it is low in sodium. Again, I cannot stress enough the importance of reading nutrition labels.

Some of these sneaky sodium-smuggling foods include:

- Bouillon cubes and seasoning packets

- Canned, packaged, or concentrated chicken, beef, or vegetable stocks

- Condiments and sauces, particularly soy sauce, salad dressings, hot sauce, pickled foods, and pasta sauce

- Canned foods, frozen meals, and instant noodles

- Cured meats like bacon, sausage, hot dogs, and deli meat

- Dairy products, especially cheese

- Packaged bread, bagels, English muffins, tortillas, and other baked goods

Sea salt, kosher salt, pink Himalayan salt, black magic salt from a secret ocean in Oz … it doesn't matter how it's marketed as "natural" or less processed; it is still salt and contains about as much sodium as regular iodized table salt.

"Plumping" is the practice of injecting salt water into meat, most often chicken and other poultry. Although this practice can be controversial, it is used to enhance the flavor and tenderness of the meat. However, introducing a saline solution can drastically increase the sodium content of these products. You need to be on the lookout and avoid meats labeled as "enhanced" with chicken broth or ones with a percentage of a salt-containing solution.

KNOW YOUR BRANDS

Reading every label at the grocery store may seem daunting in the beginning. Your first few trips to the grocery store might take you longer than usual. After a few extended trips investigating the aisles, you will learn which brands are lowest in sodium. Over time, you'll get back to shopping like you're on *Supermarket Sweep*.

Keep an eye out for foods labeled as "natural" or "organic." Products marketed with these terms tend to use fewer additives and preservatives than their traditional counterparts and, as a result, tend to be lower in sodium. Additives and preservatives usually contain sodium. However, just because a food is listed as organic or natural does not mean it is low in sodium. It is still important to read labels and compare the sodium content between all available brands.

Potassium Chloride

Potassium chloride is a compound commonly used in light sodium or sodium-free products. Potassium chloride has a salty taste, but it doesn't contain sodium.

For most, potassium chloride isn't harmful, and it may be beneficial for someone with elevated blood pressure. However, if you have kidney disease or any other disease that requires a low-*potassium* diet, you should avoid salt substitutes with potassium chloride. Besides salt substitutes, small amounts of potassium chloride can be found in many other products, such as snack bars, canned soups and sauces, potato chips, frozen entrées, cereal, condiments, and more. I've taken the time to label recipes in this book as low potassium if they have less than 500mg per serving.

Flavor Strategies in a Salt-Free Zone

It's common to get in the routine of eating and preparing the same foods. You may be open to making changes to how you cook, but you don't know where to start. One of the best places to start is by establishing a well-stocked pantry and spice cabinet. Let me share some of my favorite techniques for adding flavor without adding salt.

CITRUS JUICE AND ZEST

Citrus fruits are a treasure trove of flavor from their juice to their rind! Citrus provides a tart, acidic taste. Lemon and lime are popular citrus fruits, but you can also experiment with others, such as orange, tangerine, or grapefruit.

- Use the juice and the zest! Zest is finely grated rind and is more concentrated than the juice. You can find zesters at most home goods stores. Remember to zest your citrus before cutting and juicing it.

- Use zests when you want to add flavor without adding liquid or overpowering your dish with acidity.

- Take time to remove the seeds. I find it easiest to juice the fruit and then strain out the seeds.

- Be careful when adding citrus to dairy-based sauces, as too much can cause them to curdle.

VINEGARS

Acids like vinegar trick your brain into tasting saltier flavor without adding sodium. Adding a spoonful of vinegar to a sauce can sharpen and brighten the flavor. Vinegar comes in many varieties. Each has a unique flavor, but they all pack a punch that wakes up your taste buds. Which vinegar to use depends on the flavor profile of the dish you are making.

- Try mixing vinegar with citrus or other acids; think lemon vinaigrette.

- Sprinkle vinegar on cooked vegetables to add a tangy flavor.

- Make your own salad dressings by mixing vinegar with olive oil.

- Use vinegar to quickly pickle your own onions and cucumbers without adding salt. Just soak them in some apple cider vinegar and a couple teaspoons of sugar for at least an hour.

SPICES

Despite the name, not all spices are spicy. A spice can be a seed (mustard), root (ginger), fruit (cayenne pepper), bark (cinnamon), or other plant material (like cloves, which are flower buds). These items are typically dried and ground into powdery substances. Spices have added potent flavors to bland food for thousands of years.

- A little goes a long way! Be careful when adding spices because things can get intense fast. Start with a small amount like ⅛ teaspoon, taste test, and then add more as desired.

- Make your own spice mixes without the sodium. Read the ingredients of your favorite spice blends to figure out which spices to mix; just leave out the salt.

HERBS AND AROMATICS

Like spices, herbs are plant parts—leaves, flowers, or stems—used for flavoring. They can be used dried or fresh and are sodium-free.

- For the best flavor, add dried herbs during cooking and fresh herbs at the end.

- Freeze fresh herbs to keep them longer.

- Try growing your own herb garden. Many herbs are easy to grow right on your windowsill.

- If substituting fresh for dried herbs, use 1½ times the amount; if substituting dried for fresh, use ¾ of the amount.

- Some herbs have more intense flavors than others, so start with less and increase to taste.
  - » High-intensity herbs: tarragon, bay leaves, rosemary, sage, mint, thyme, lavender
  - » Low-intensity herbs: dill, basil, chives, parsley, oregano

LOW-SODIUM AND SALT-FREE SNACKS

Traditional snack foods, like chips, cookies, and crackers, can be loaded with salt. Even naturally low-sodium snacks like nuts can have high amounts of sodium added to them. Keeping a selection of flavorful snacks on hand can help reduce your sodium intake. Some of my favorites include:

- Apple and no-salt-added peanut butter

- Carrot or celery sticks with low-sodium ranch dressing

- Dried fruit without sugar added

- Fresh fruit and Greek yogurt

- Grape tomatoes and sliced cucumber with low-sodium hummus

- Roasted chickpeas, soybeans, and seeds without added salt

- Unsalted nuts

- Unsalted popcorn

Stocking Your Low-Sodium Kitchen

Keep these staples around the house for building easy, low-sodium meals.

For the Pantry

Seasonings and Condiments

- Dried herbs: basil, parsley, thyme, rosemary, oregano, dill, bay leaves (remove before eating)
- Honey
- Low-sodium chicken and vegetable broth
- Low-sodium soy sauce
- Oils: extra-virgin olive oil, sesame oil, vegetable oil, sunflower oil, avocado oil
- Pure maple syrup
- Spices: garlic powder, black pepper, red pepper flakes, cumin, turmeric, paprika, dry mustard, ground sodium-free spice blends
- Vinegar: red wine, apple cider, balsamic, rice

Fruits and Vegetables

- Bananas
- Crushed or chunk pineapple in 100 percent fruit juice
- Mixed fruit cups in 100 percent fruit juice
- No-salt-added canned or jarred diced tomatoes, tomato sauce, and tomato paste
- No-salt-added canned vegetables: green beans, peas and carrots, artichoke hearts, mushrooms, mixed vegetables
- No-sugar-added applesauce
- No-sugar-added dried fruits like raisins or dried cranberries
- Onions
- Potatoes: fresh or canned without salt added

CONTINUED

Grains and Starches

- No-salt-added canned corn
- Quick oats
- Unsalted popcorn or pop-corn kernels
- Whole-grain cereal or granola (aim for less than 10g added sugar)
- Whole grains including brown rice, wild rice, quinoa, amaranth, farro, barley, spelt, millet, bulgur, or buckwheat
- Whole-wheat pasta

Proteins

- Dried beans or no-salt-added canned beans including black, white, kidney, navy, pinto, and chickpeas
- No-salt-added canned tuna packed in water
- Other legumes such as lentils, split peas, or mung beans
- Soy milk or other nondairy milk
- Unsalted nut butter
- Unsalted nuts including almonds, walnuts, cashews, peanuts, maca-damia, or pistachios
- Unsalted seeds such as sunflower, flaxseed, chia, or pumpkin

——————— For the Refrigerator ———————

Seasonings and Condiments

- Fresh herbs: basil, mint, dill, thyme
- Low-sodium mayonnaise
- Low-sodium salad dressings
- Minced garlic in olive oil
- No-salt-added ketchup and mustard

Fruits and Vegetables

- Fresh fruit: lemons, limes, grape-fruits, apples, oranges, plums, tangerines, grapes, berries, sliced pineapple, melons

- Fresh sliced vegetables for snacking: celery, carrots, cucumbers, red peppers, grape tomatoes

Grains and Starches

- Low-sodium whole-wheat bread, English muffins, and pitas

- Whole-grain wraps or tortillas

Proteins and Dairy

- Eggs
- Greek yogurt
- Low-sodium hummus

- Low-sodium nitrate- and sulfate-free turkey or ham

For the Freezer

Seasonings and Condiments

- Unsalted butter—can be frozen for up to 5 months

Fruits and Vegetables

- Frozen fruit: berries, pineapple, mangoes, mixed fruits

- Frozen vegetables: broccoli, peas, carrots, spinach, cauliflower

CONTINUED

Grains and Starches

- Frozen corn
- Frozen potatoes

Proteins and Dairy

- Boneless, skinless chicken breasts and/or thighs
- Edamame (soybeans), shelled and in the pod
- Fish fillets
- Lean ground turkey or beef
- Pork chops

Why Meal Prep?

Meal prepping refers to the practice of preparing and/or portioning large quantities of food at one time for future consumption. Some may cook in bulk and store food cafeteria-style, meaning individual items are prepared, kept separate until mealtime, and then quickly combined for an easy meal. Alternatively, I will teach you the most popular method of meal preparation, which is to pre-portion servings in individual containers for a grab-and-go meal. There are many advantages to this kind of meal prep.

YOU CONTROL WHAT'S IN THE FOOD. When you cook, you control what goes into your food, particularly how much salt or sodium is added.

YOU CONTROL THE PORTIONS. You control how much food you eat at every meal. Meal prep is great for monitoring portions and reducing food waste.

ALL THE CONVENIENCE WITHOUT THE CONVENIENCE FOODS. Meal prepping at home can save time and prevent last-minute bad decisions on busy days when you don't have time or simply don't feel like cooking.

HEALTHY EATING ON A BUDGET. Meal prepping allows you to choose seasonal ingredients and other budget-friendly options, reduce waste, and keep average meal costs to a minimum.

Six-Step Prep

Follow these six simple steps to meal prep success! A little organization can go a long way and save a lot of time preparing meals ahead for the week.

1. **CHOOSE YOUR PREP DAY(S)**

   Decide when you're going to perform your meal prep. In the beginning, I recommend setting aside two to three hours a week to complete all your prep. The more experience you get, the more efficient you will be. Eventually, you will need to set aside less time each week to plan and prepare your meals.

2. **MAKE YOUR PLAN**

   Once you've decided on your meal prep day, the next step is creating your meal plan and shopping list. In this book, I've provided you with plans, including shopping lists, to help you develop your own plans in the future. When developing your own plan:

   » Choose three to six recipes with at least one recipe for breakfast, lunch, and dinner every week.

   » Aim for at least three or four servings per recipe, depending on how many days you plan to eat that dish.

   » Look for recipes that use similar ingredients so they can do double duty.

3. **GO GROCERY SHOPPING**

   Now that you have a plan and grocery list, you need to decide when to shop. Remember, in the beginning, shopping may take longer, so plan accordingly. Also, depending on where you live, you may need to go to multiple locations to obtain all the items you need.

4. **PREPARE AND COOK**

   When it comes time to cook, start by setting up your mise en place. This French culinary term refers to setting up all your equipment and prepping your ingredients—chopping, peeling, measuring—before cooking. Having everything at your fingertips makes cooking easier and saves time overall.

5. **PORTION AND PACK**

Have your containers clean and dry so you can portion recipe items immediately. Portion heated foods into containers so they cool faster. Be sure to
let all items cool to room temperature before storing them in the refrigerator or freezer. To avoid spoilage, store cooled items immediately.

6. **GRAB AND GO**

Store meals in the refrigerator if you plan to use them within the next few
days. Otherwise, store them in the freezer for an easy meal in the future.

Storage Essentials

Proper storage is key to successful meal prepping. Let's dive deeper into the tools
needed to properly store your culinary creations.

STORAGE CONTAINERS

The type of storage containers you use is personal preference. For the weekly recipes in this book, you will need at least 21 individual containers (3 meals x 7 days).
Here are some options so you can make the best decision for yourself.

Plastic versus Glass

There are advantages and disadvantages to both plastic and glass containers.

Plastic is lightweight and not as fragile as glass. Some controversy exists
over whether heated plastics can leach harmful chemicals into foods. However,
most experts feel that plastics marked as microwave-safe do not pose a risk to
your health.

Glass containers may be better for your health, but they are heavier. Always
make sure glass containers cool slowly to prevent cracking. You also need to purchase glass that can go in the freezer.

Size and Shape

I like to use a variety of containers in different shapes and sizes. For this book, I
recommend 7 or 8 (16- to 20-ounce) round containers or mason jars, 13 to 14 (25- to
30-ounce) square or rectangular containers, and 4 to 8 (2- to 3-ounce) containers.

Single versus Multi-Compartment

Once again, the choice here is mostly personal preference. For some recipes, you may want to keep foods separate to preserve freshness or keep flavors apart.

SAFE STORAGE

No one wants food poisoning, so it is essential to store foods safely to avoid getting sick. Here are my top tips for safe storage and information on when to throw food away.

In the Refrigerator

- Make sure the temperature is at or below 40°F (4°C). Check regularly.

- Store items toward the back of the refrigerator where it's colder and the temperature is most consistent.

- Store prepared meals above any raw meat or eggs.

- If a prepared meal looks or smells bad, throw it out. Visible mold is a sign that food has spoiled.

In the Freezer

- Make sure temperature is at or below 0°F (−18°C). Check regularly.

- Label and date foods before freezing.

- Leave extra space, or headroom, in the top of the container to account for food expansion when frozen.

- Freezer burn is an indicator of food quality, not food safety. It causes dry spots in the food but isn't dangerous.

REHEATING

Your dish may have tasted perfect before storing it, but the reheating process can create dry, overcooked food if you're not careful. Glass containers can be reheated in the microwave or oven, but food stored in plastic needs to be transferred to another dish before reheating in the oven. I will provide you with my best tips and tricks for reheating dishes throughout the book so they taste the same as or even better than the day you made them.

About the Meal Prep Plans

Each week of meal prep has its own chapter as well as an overarching theme. Each theme introduces various healthy eating concepts. These concepts work along with a low-sodium diet to improve your overall health and reduce your risk of developing certain health conditions like heart disease, kidney disease, and diabetes. Incorporating these different concepts may prevent your disease from worsening If you already have one or more of these conditions.

These six plans will teach you how meal prep works. Every weekly prep includes a shopping list, instructions to efficiently execute the prep, and the recipes included in the week. I hope that once you cook your way through the six weekly plans I have created, you will develop the confidence to mix and match your own combinations.

About the Recipes

I chose these recipes to be easy and efficient, and, at the same time, to teach you how to infuse flavor without salt. Since individual tastes vary, I was conservative with my measurements of spices and herbs. Feel free to add more (or less) to your liking!

For the cook's convenience, I highlighted prep time, cook time, yield, or number of servings, and how long meals will last in the refrigerator and the freezer, if freezer-friendly. The calories in each recipe vary from about 300 to 600. Since everyone's caloric needs are different, you may need to include one to three snacks, such as those on page 12, in your daily intake to feel satisfied.

RECIPE LABELS

I've added labels to identify recipes in this book that meet specific dietary restrictions or preferences, including:

DAIRY-FREE Does not contain milk from any animal or by-products of animal milk

GLUTEN-FREE Does not contain wheat, barley, rye, or gluten-containing ingredients (always make sure to check the ingredient packaging, in order to ensure foods—especially oats , which are naturally gluten-free—were processed in a completely gluten-free facility)

LOW POTASSIUM Total potassium per serving is less than 550mg

VEGAN Does not contain any animal products or by-products (All vegan recipes are also vegetarian and dairy-free)

VEGETARIAN Does not contain meat, poultry, or fish

SODIUM CONTENT

Recipes in this book will not contain more than 500mg of sodium per serving. For easy reference, each recipe has an icon indicating its level of salt.

LOW SODIUM 250mg to 500mg

LOWER SODIUM 50mg to 249mg

LOWEST SODIUM 0mg to 49mg

NUTRITIONAL INFORMATION AND TIPS

Each recipe includes nutritional information, including calories, total fat (g), saturated fat (g), protein (g), carbohydrates (g), sugar (g), fiber (g), sodium (mg), calcium (mg), and potassium (mg). There are also tips for reheating, preparing, and storing ingredients; alternative ingredients; and cooking methods.

CHAPTER TWO

Week 1: Heart-Healthy Fats

Fat-free and low-fat products were all the rage in the '90s, but now we understand that fat is not the enemy. An extensive review of available studies performed in 2018 found that certain types of fat, called "monounsaturated" (MUFA) and "polyunsaturated" (PUFA), may reduce your risk of developing heart disease. This week's theme focuses on foods that are high in mono- and polyunsaturated fatty acids, like avocados, olive oil, walnuts, chia seeds, and salmon.

To reduce waste, these ingredients are used in multiple dishes in this chapter and throughout the rest of the book. You may have to invest in some of the pantry items up front, but most of these items will last you a while and provide the basics for sodium-free cooking long after you finish the recipes in this book.

Recipe List

Shopping List

Pantry Items

- Black pepper

- Brown rice (14 ounces)

- Chia seeds (5 ounces)

- Curry powder, sodium-free

- Dijon mustard (8 ounces)

- Garlic, minced in oil (1 [16-ounce] container)

- Honey (4 ounces)

- Italian seasoning, sodium-free

- Olive oil (8 ounces)

- Penne or fusilli, whole-wheat (1 pound)

- Pineapple in 100 percent fruit juice (1 [20-ounce] can)

- Red wine vinegar (8 ounces)

- Soy sauce, low-sodium (4 ounces)

- Vanilla extract (2 ounces)

- Walnuts, unsalted (10 ounces)

Produce

- Asparagus (1 bunch)

- Avocados (2)

- Bananas (2)

- Bell pepper, red (1)

- Berries (2 cups)

- Carrot (1)

- Lemons (2)

- Lime (1)

- Onion, red (1)

- Spinach, baby (10 ounces)

- Thyme, fresh (1 bunch)

- Tomatoes, cherry (2 pints)

- Zucchini (1)

Meat and Seafood

- Chicken breast, boneless, skinless (1½ pounds)
- Salmon fillets, skinless (4) (1 pound)

Dairy and Eggs

- Feta cheese (2 ounces)

Frozen

- Edamame, shelled, no-salt-added (1 [16-ounce] bag or 1 [16-ounce] can)

Be Sure to Have on Hand

- 2 large baking sheets or roasting pans
- 2 large saucepans (at least 2-quart) with lids
- 12-inch skillet
- Blender
- Chef's knife
- Colander
- Cutting board
- Measuring cups and spoons

- Mixing bowls: 2 small and 2 medium to large
- Parchment paper
- Storage containers
  - » 21 (20- to 25-ounce) containers including:
    - » 3 containers with 2 divided sections
    - » 3 mason jars
    - » 4 gallon-size plastic seal-able bags
- Whisk

Week 1

	Breakfast	Lunch	Dinner
Day 1	Berry Nut Chia Seed Pudding	Walnut and Feta Pasta Salad	Lemon Pepper Salmon Pack
Day 2	Spinach and Avocado Smoothie Pack	Curry Chicken Stir-Fry	Garlic Herb Chicken Pack
Day 3	Berry Nut Chia Seed Pudding	Walnut and Feta Pasta Salad	Lemon Pepper Salmon Pack
Day 4	Spinach and Avocado Smoothie Pack	Walnut and Feta Pasta Salad	Garlic Herb Chicken Pack
Day 5	Berry Nut Chia Seed Pudding	Curry Chicken Stir-Fry	Lemon Pepper Salmon Pack
Day 6	Spinach and Avocado Smoothie Pack	Curry Chicken Stir-Fry	Garlic Herb Chicken Pack
Day 7	Spinach and Avocado Smoothie Pack	Curry Chicken Stir-Fry	Lemon Pepper Salmon Pack

Step-by-Step Meal Prep

1. Preheat the oven to 400°F.

2. Make the rice for the Curry Chicken Stir-Fry (page 31) and Lemon Pepper Salmon Pack (page 33).

3. Cook the pasta for the Walnut and Feta Pasta Salad (page 30) and Garlic Herb Chicken Pack (page 35).

4. While rice and pasta are cooking, continue preparing the Salmon Packs through step 7 and the Garlic Herb Chicken packs through step 4. I recommend setting multiple timers because each pack needs to cook a different amount of time.

5. While the packs bake, preheat a medium frying pan on the stove, and complete the Curry Chicken Stir-Fry.

6. Once the pasta has finished cooking, assemble the Walnut and Feta Pasta Salad.

7. While everything cools, make the Berry Nut Chia Seed Pudding (page 28) and the Spinach and Avocado Smoothie Pack (page 29).

8. Once everything is cooked and cooled, portion, pack, label, and store your meals for the week! Freeze all the Spinach and Avocado Smoothie Pack portions, two portions of Curry Chicken Stir-Fry, one portion of Lemon Pepper Salmon Pack, and one portion of Garlic Herb Chicken Pack. Store everything else in the refrigerator.

Berry Nut Chia Seed Pudding

PREP TIME: 5 minutes, plus overnight to set | **SERVES** 3
REFRIGERATOR: Up to 5 days | **FREEZER:** Up to 3 weeks

Chia seeds are a great source of healthy omega-3 fats as well as protein and fiber. This simple recipe additionally incorporates soy milk and walnuts, which both provide healthy polyunsaturated fats.

1½ cups soy milk
6 tablespoon chia seeds
2 tablespoons honey

¼ teaspoon vanilla extract
2 cups fresh berries
½ cup chopped walnuts

1. In a medium bowl, whisk the milk, chia seeds, honey, and vanilla until smooth. Divide the mixture evenly among 3 mason jars and store in the refrigerator overnight to set.
2. Before eating, top each serving with a third of the berries and a third of the walnuts. Stir well.

PREP TIP: Some find it easier to combine the milk and seed mixture in a large bowl in the refrigerator for a few hours to thicken before stirring and dividing into individual containers and adding toppings.

VARIATION: Use any milk alternative to keep this recipe dairy-free. You can create variations of this pudding using different fruit and nuts. Fresh fruit can be substituted with frozen, but be sure to thaw it and drain the excess liquid first.

Calories: 425; Total fat: 25g; Saturated fat: 3g; Sodium: 70mg; Carbohydrates: 44g; Fiber: 15g; Protein: 12g; Calcium: 349mg; Potassium: 447mg

Spinach and Avocado Smoothie Pack

PREP TIME: 10 minutes | **SERVES** 4 | **REFRIGERATOR:** Up to 2 days
FREEZER: Recommended, up to 3 months

Make-ahead freezer packs are ideal for a fast breakfast. Avocado is a great source of monounsaturated fats and gives smoothies a nice creamy texture.

2 medium ripe avocados, halved, pitted, and peeled
2 medium bananas, halved
4 cups fresh baby spinach

1 (20-ounce) can sliced pineapple in 100 percent fruit juice, drained
¼ cup chia seeds
6 cups soy milk
1 to 2 tablespoons honey (optional)

1. In each of the 4 (1-gallon) plastic freezer bags or airtight containers, combine half an avocado, half a banana, 1 cup of spinach, a quarter of the pineapple, and 1 tablespoon of chia seeds.
2. Seal, label, and freeze until ready to blend.
3. To serve, transfer the contents of one smoothie pack to a blender with 1½ cups of soy milk and 1 to 2 teaspoons of honey (if using). Blend until smooth and then serve in your favorite to-go container!

VARIATION: Replace the spinach with other greens like kale, but avoid the extremely bitter ones like arugula. You can also use fresh pineapple or try apples or mangoes instead to add sweetness.

Calories: 473; Total fat: 26g; Saturated fat: 3g; Sodium: 162mg; Carbohydrates: 52g; Fiber: 17g; Protein: 17g; Calcium: 600mg; Potassium: 1,504mg

Walnut and Feta Pasta Salad

PREP TIME: 10 minutes | **COOK TIME:** 15 minutes | **SERVES** 3
REFRIGERATOR: Up to 5 days | **FREEZER:** Not recommended

Walnuts add a nice crunch to this pasta salad and are a great source of polyunsaturated fats!

8 ounces whole-wheat penne or fusilli pasta
2 tablespoons olive oil
2 tablespoons red wine vinegar
1 teaspoon minced garlic
1 teaspoon Dijon mustard

½ teaspoon freshly ground black pepper
⅓ red onion, diced
1 cup cherry tomatoes, halved
2 cups chopped fresh baby spinach
¾ cup chopped walnuts
½ cup crumbled feta cheese

1. Make the pasta according to the package directions. Strain, rinse with cold water, and transfer the noodles to a large bowl.
2. While the pasta cooks, whisk the olive oil, vinegar, garlic, mustard, and pepper in a small bowl.
3. Add the dressing, onion, tomatoes, spinach, walnuts, and feta cheese to the pasta and portion into 3 containers.

PREP TIP: Although toasting the walnuts is not necessary for this recipe, doing so adds another layer of flavor. Toast walnuts in a dry medium skillet over medium-high heat for 1 to 2 minutes.

Calories: 623; Total fat: 35g; Saturated fat: 7g; Sodium: 274mg; Carbohydrates: 66g; Fiber: 10g; Protein: 20g; Calcium: 213mg; Potassium: 564mg

Curry Chicken Stir-Fry

PREP TIME: 30 minutes | **COOK TIME:** 55 minutes | **SERVES** 4
REFRIGERATOR: Up to 5 days | **FREEZER:** Up to 6 months

Although soy sauce is notoriously high in sodium, whole soybeans are naturally sodium-free and a great source of healthy fats. "Lite" soy sauce can still contain a fair amount of sodium, so use it sparingly!

FOR THE RICE

2 cups brown rice
4 cups water

1 tablespoon olive oil

FOR THE STIR-FRY

1 tablespoon olive oil
1 tablespoon low-sodium
  soy sauce
1 tablespoon minced garlic
1 tablespoon sodium-free curry
  powder, divided
Juice of 1 lime

2 boneless, skinless chicken breasts
  (about ½ pound), cut into strips or
  1-inch chunks
1 red bell pepper, cut into strips
⅔ red onion, diced (about 1 cup)
1 cup shelled edamame, frozen
  and defrosted or canned with
  no salt added

TO MAKE THE RICE

1. In a medium saucepan, combine the rice, water, and olive oil. Bring to a boil over medium-high heat. Cover, reduce the heat to low, and cook for 35 to 45 minutes until all the liquid is absorbed. Turn off the heat and let the rice stand for 20 minutes. Let it cool, then set aside half for the Lemon Pepper Salmon Pack (page 33). Divide the remaining rice among 4 containers.

CONTINUED

TO MAKE THE STIR-FRY

2. While the rice cooks, in a medium bowl, whisk together the olive oil, soy sauce, garlic, 2 teaspoons of curry powder, and 1 tablespoon of lime juice. Add the chicken and turn to coat it in the marinade.
3. In a separate medium bowl, toss the bell pepper, onion, and edamame with the remaining 1 teaspoon of curry powder.
4. Place a large skillet over medium heat and sauté the chicken and marinade until the chicken is white on the outside, 4 to 5 minutes. Add the onion mixture and cook for another 3 to 4 minutes until the onions become translucent.
5. Remove the skillet from the heat. Divide the stir-fry into the 4 containers on top of the rice.

REHEAT: In the microwave, heat partially covered on high in 30-second intervals, stirring occasionally, until heated through. Alternatively, transfer the stir-fry and rice to a medium skillet over medium heat and cook for 2 to 3 minutes, stirring occasionally.

VARIATION: Skip the meat completely—add extra vegetables like broccoli and mushrooms or use drained, cubed tofu in place of an animal protein! Cooking times may vary by a few minutes.

Nutrition: Calories: 371; Total fat: 11g; Saturated fat: 2g; Sodium: 166mg; Carbohydrates: 48g; Fiber: 6g; Protein: 22g; Calcium: 66mg; Potassium: 643mg

Lemon Pepper Salmon Pack

PREP TIME: 30 minutes | **COOK TIME:** 15 minutes | **SERVES** 4
REFRIGERATOR: Up to 5 days | **FREEZER:** Up to 6 months

Fish, particularly salmon, contains omega-3 fatty acids, which are a type of polyunsaturated fats. Packs are one of the easiest types of meals to prep ahead because everything is already individually portioned and cooks together with little to no cleanup!

**Rice set aside from Curry Chicken
  Stir-Fry (page 31)**
1 lemon
1 medium zucchini, julienned
1 medium carrot, julienned

4 (4-ounce) salmon fillets
2 tablespoons olive oil
**½ teaspoon freshly ground
  black pepper**
1 teaspoon fresh thyme leaves

1. Divide the prepared rice among 4 containers.
2. Preheat the oven to 400°F. Measure and cut 4 (12-by-18-inch) sheets of parchment paper.
3. Zest the lemon and cut it in half. Juice half (reserving the juice) and cut the remaining half into 4 slices.
4. On a sheet of parchment paper, lay a quarter of the zucchini and carrots; then top with a salmon fillet. Repeat to make 4 packets.
5. In a small bowl, whisk the olive oil, lemon juice, 1 teaspoon of lemon zest, and pepper. Divide the mixture among the packets, place a lemon slice on each salmon fillet, and sprinkle with the thyme.
6. Close the packets by bringing up the 2 sides to meet, folding over the edges about half an inch, and then folding again. Leave some space inside for heat circulation and expansion. Close the ends tightly so no liquid drips out. Transfer the packs to a baking sheet.
7. Bake for 10 to 12 minutes, or until the salmon is flaky but still bright pink in the center. Remove from the oven and—making sure to use oven mitts—open the packs immediately to let out the steam and prevent the salmon from overcooking. Allow to cool. Top the rice in each container with the contents of a pack.

CONTINUED

REHEAT: In the microwave, heat on high in 30-second intervals, rotating the plate in between, until the fish reaches an internal temperature of 145°F. To use the oven, place in an oven-safe dish and heat at 350°F for 5 to 10 minutes. If frozen, you can thaw in the refrigerator overnight or heat directly from the freezer.

PREP TIP: It's best to undercook salmon when meal prepping so it does not overcook during the reheating process.

VARIATION: You can make numerous variations of this dish by mixing different types of fish, vegetables, and grains. Try mahi-mahi with broccoli and quinoa! It's also good with a variety of citrus fruits; if you have grapefruit or orange try those in place of the lemon.

Calories: 424; Total fat: 17g; Saturated fat: 3g; Sodium: 68mg; Carbohydrates: 40g; Fiber: 3g; Protein: 27g; Calcium: 39mg; Potassium: 849mg

Garlic Herb Chicken Pack

PREP TIME: 30 minutes | **COOK TIME:** 45 minutes | **SERVES** 3
REFRIGERATOR: Up to 5 days | **FREEZER:** Up to 6 months

Packs can be made in endless combinations and are a fast and easy way to meal prep. This recipe shows another variation using chicken breasts, asparagus, tomatoes, and pasta.

8 ounces whole-wheat penne or
   fusilli pasta
1 bunch asparagus (about 12 stalks),
   woody ends removed
1 pint cherry tomatoes, halved
3 boneless, skinless chicken breasts
   (about ¾ pound)

2 tablespoons olive oil
1 tablespoon red wine vinegar
1 tablespoon sodium-free Italian
   seasoning
1 tablespoon freshly squeezed
   lemon juice

1. Make the pasta according to the package directions. Strain, rinse with cold water, divide among 3 containers, and set aside.
2. Preheat the oven to 400°F.
3. Measure and cut 3 (12-by-18-inch) pieces of parchment paper. Evenly divide the asparagus and tomatoes among the parchment paper and top each with a chicken breast.
4. In a small bowl, whisk the olive oil, vinegar, Italian seasoning, and lemon juice. Pour the mixture over the chicken and vegetables. Fold the parchment paper by bringing up 2 sides to meet, folding over the edges about half an inch, and then folding again. Leave some room inside for heat circulation and expansion. Close the ends tightly so no liquid drips out.
5. Place the packs on a baking sheet and bake for 25 to 30 minutes. Use oven mitts to open the packs immediately after removing them from oven to prevent the chicken from overcooking. Allow to cool.
6. Top the pasta in each container with the contents of a pack.

CONTINUED

REHEAT: To reheat in the microwave, separate the chicken from the veggies and pasta. Reheat the chicken on high for 60 seconds and then in 30-second intervals, rotating the plate in between, until the chicken reaches an internal temperature of 165°F. Add 1 teaspoon of water to the veggies and pasta. Microwave on high in 30-second intervals, stirring in between, until heated through. To use the oven, place in an oven-safe dish, add 1 tablespoon of water, and cover. Heat at 350°F for 5 to 10 minutes. If frozen, you can thaw in the refrigerator overnight or heat directly from the freezer.

PREP TIP: Use a divided storage container to keep the chicken separate from the vegetables and pasta. This will make reheating easier.

Calories: 339; Total fat: 15g; Saturated fat: 3g; Sodium: 232mg; Carbohydrates: 18g; Fiber: 5g; Protein: 32g; Calcium: 45mg; Potassium: 783mg

CHAPTER THREE

Week 2: High-Fiber Whole Grains

Fiber is a carbohydrate that the human body cannot digest. It is found in plant foods like vegetables, fruits, and whole grains. Fiber is important for many reasons, including slowing down how quickly the body digests carbs and keeping bowel movements regular. Refined or processed carbohydrates contain little to no fiber; whole grains, on the other hand, are naturally high in fiber as well as important micronutrients. Two reviews of available scientific studies published in the *Journal of Chiropractic Medicine* in 2017 and the *European Journal of Epidemiology* in 2014 concluded that high-fiber diets may reduce the risk of heart disease and diabetes. The recipes in this chapter highlight some of my favorite whole grains: oats, quinoa, farro, and corn.

Recipe List

SHOPPING LIST

Pantry Items

- Almonds, sliced (5 ounces)
- Balsamic vinegar (8 ounces)
- Bay leaf, whole (1)
- Black beans, no-salt-added (1 [15-ounce] can)
- Black pepper
- Cayenne pepper
- Cumin, ground
- Dijon mustard (8 ounces)
- Farro, whole or semi-pearled (1 pound)
- Garlic, minced in oil (1 [16-ounce] container)
- Honey (4 ounces)
- Italian seasoning, sodium-free
- Oats, quick (10 ounces)
- Olive oil (8 ounces)
- Quinoa (6 ounces)
- Tomatoes, diced with green chiles, no-salt-added (2 [10-ounce] cans)
- Tortillas, corn (6)
- Vanilla extract (2 ounces)

Produce

- Bananas (3)
- Basil, fresh (1 bunch)
- Bell pepper, red (1)
- Broccoli (2 or 3 heads)
- Cherries (1 pound)
- Cilantro, fresh (1 bunch)
- Green cabbage (1 head) or bag of chopped green/purple cabbage
- Jalapeño pepper (1)
- Lime (1)
- Onions (2)
- Peaches (2)
- Spinach, baby (10 ounces)
- Tomatoes, Roma or plum (8)

Meat and Seafood

- Pork, shoulder, butt, or tenderloin (2 pounds)
- Turkey, lean ground (1 pound)

Dairy and Eggs

- Eggs, large (6)
- Feta cheese, crumbled (8 ounces)
- Greek yogurt, plain (30 ounces)
- Milk, low-fat, or milk alternative of choice (1 quart)

Be Sure to Have on Hand

- 2 large baking sheets or roasting pans
- 2 large saucepans (at least 2-quart) with lids
- 12-inch nonstick skillet
- Chef's knife
- Colander or strainer
- Cutting board
- Measuring cups and spoons
- Mixing bowls
- Muffin tin

- Rubber spatula
- Slow cooker, large stockpot, or Dutch oven
- Storage containers
  » 21 (20- to 25-ounce) containers including:
    » 3 containers with 3 divided sections
    » 3 small containers 2 to 3 ounces in size
    » 4 mason jars
- Whisk

Week 2

	Breakfast	Lunch	Dinner
Day 1	Cherry Banana Overnight Oatmeal	Peach and Feta Farro Salad	Pork Burrito Bowl
Day 2	Cherry Banana Overnight Oatmeal	Peach and Feta Farro Salad	Mini Turkey Meatloaf
Day 3	Cherry Banana Overnight Oatmeal	Peach and Feta Farro Salad	Pork Burrito Bowl
Day 4	Cherry Banana Overnight Oatmeal	Peach and Feta Farro Salad	Mini Turkey Meatloaf
Day 5	Quinoa Scramble	Pork Carnitas Tacos	Pork Burrito Bowl
Day 6	Quinoa Scramble	Pork Carnitas Tacos	Mini Turkey Meatloaf
Day 7	Quinoa Scramble	Pork Carnitas Tacos	Mini Turkey Meatloaf

Step-by-Step Meal Prep

1. Preheat the oven to 400°F.

2. Make the pork for the Pork Carnitas Tacos (page 50) and Pork Burrito Bowl (page 52).

3. Once the pork is cooking, cook the farro for Peach and Farro Salad (page 48) and the Mini Turkey Meatloaves (page 53).

4. Make the Mini Turkey Meatloaves through step 4.

5. Make the Quinoa Scramble (page 45), setting aside the quinoa and black beans and pico de gallo for the Pork Burrito Bowls and Pork Carnitas Tacos.

6. Complete the Cherry Banana Overnight Oatmeal (page 44).

7. After the farro has cooked and cooled, make the Peach and Feta Farro Salad.

8. Once the pork is cooked, complete the Pork Carnitas Tacos and the Pork Burrito Bowls.

9. Wait until everything has cooled to room temperature. Then portion, pack, label, and store! Freeze two portions of Quinoa Scramble, two portions of Mini Turkey Meatloaves, and two portions of Pork Carnitas Tacos.

Cherry Banana Overnight Oatmeal

PREP TIME: 10 minutes, plus overnight to chill | **SERVES** 4
REFRIGERATOR: Up to 5 days | **FREEZER:** Up to 3 months

Oatmeal is an amazing grain with many nutrients to offer, but it can get boring. Leaving oats to soak overnight eliminates the need for cooking and offers an alternative to traditional oatmeal. Adding fruit like cherries and bananas can provide tartness and sweetness with natural sugars.

2 cups quick oats
2 cups plain Greek yogurt
2 cups low-fat milk
3 bananas (2 mashed, 1 sliced)
8 teaspoons honey

½ teaspoon vanilla extract
1 cup halved and pitted cherries
2 to 4 tablespoons sliced almonds
   (optional)

1. Evenly divide the quick oats, yogurt, milk, mashed banana, honey, and vanilla among 4 mason jars.
2. Top each with a quarter of the cherries, sliced bananas, and almonds (if using). Refrigerate overnight.

REHEAT: Though this oatmeal can be eaten as is, you can make it taste like bread right out of the oven by warming it up in the microwave on high in 20-second intervals, stirring in between.

VARIATION: There are endless ways to shake up your overnight oats recipe by mixing in different fresh or dried fruits, nuts, nut butter, seeds, and even chocolate chips or ground coconut. You can replace the almonds with left-over walnuts and chia seeds from week 1 if you want to save a few dollars at the store.

Calories: 473; Total fat: 10g; Saturated fat: 5g; Sodium: 116mg; Carbohydrates: 82g; Fiber: 8g; Protein: 18g; Calcium: 331mg; Potassium: 980mg

Quinoa Scramble

PREP TIME: 20 minutes | **COOK TIME:** 40 minutes | **SERVES** 3
REFRIGERATOR: Up to 5 days | **FREEZER:** Up to 3 months

Quinoa makes a great breakfast grain because it has complete protein, which means it contains the nine essential amino acids the body cannot produce on its own. It also provides healthy carbohydrates. Mixing quinoa with eggs in this recipe gives you a high-protein, fiber-packed punch of energy to start your day.

FOR THE QUINOA AND BLACK BEANS

1 cup quinoa, rinsed
1 (12-ounce) can no-salt-added diced
    tomatoes and green chiles
1 cup water
1 tablespoon minced garlic in olive oil

1 teaspoon ground cumin
¼ teaspoon cayenne pepper
1 (15-ounce) can no-salt-added black
    beans, drained and rinsed

FOR THE SCRAMBLE

1 red bell pepper, cut into ½-inch slices
1 tablespoon olive oil, divided
½ teaspoon freshly ground black
    pepper, divided

5 large eggs
¼ cup low-fat milk or soy milk
1 (10-ounce) bag spinach

FOR THE PICO DE GALLO

Juice of ½ lime
2 tablespoons chopped fresh cilantro
2 teaspoon minced garlic in olive oil
¼ teaspoon ground cumin

6 Roma or plum tomatoes, diced
½ white onion, diced
1 jalapeño pepper, diced

FOR ASSEMBLING

½ cup plain Greek yogurt

CONTINUED

TO MAKE THE QUINOA AND BLACK BEANS

1. In a medium saucepan, bring the quinoa, diced tomatoes and chiles with their juices, water, garlic, cumin, and cayenne pepper to a boil. Cover, reduce heat to low, and simmer for 15 minutes or until the liquid is absorbed.
2. When the quinoa is cooked, add the black beans. Divide the quinoa mixture in half and set aside half for the Pork Burrito Bowl (page 52).

TO MAKE THE SCRAMBLE

3. Preheat the oven to 400°F.
4. Spread the bell peppers on a baking sheet, toss with 1 teaspoon of olive oil and ¼ teaspoon of black pepper, and roast for 10 to 15 minutes until the edges start to turn brown. Remove the peppers from the oven and set aside.
5. In a large bowl, whisk the eggs, milk, and remaining ¼ teaspoon of pepper until blended. Heat the remaining 2 teaspoons of olive oil in a large nonstick skillet over medium heat. Add the egg mixture and let it sit for 1 minute. Then drag a rubber spatula along the bottom of the pan and pull up the cooked egg. Allow the liquid to fill the empty space and repeat until the eggs are fluffy and no longer liquid.
6. When the eggs are almost finished cooking, add the spinach to the skillet. Cook for 30 to 60 seconds, until wilted. Stir the spinach into the eggs and remove from heat.

TO MAKE THE PICO DE GALLO

7. In a small bowl, whisk the lime juice, cilantro, garlic, and cumin. Add the tomatoes, onion, and jalapeño and toss to mix. Set aside a third of the mixture and refrigerate the remaining two-thirds for the Pork Carnitas Tacos (page 50) and Pork Burrito Bowl (page 52).

TO ASSEMBLE

8. In 3 containers, arrange a third of the quinoa and black beans, a third of the roasted bell pepper, a third of the egg-and-spinach mixture, and ½ cup of pico de gallo. Divide the yogurt into 3 (1- to 2-ounce) containers.

REHEAT: In the microwave, heat on high in 30-second increments until warm, stirring in between. You can also try warming this up on the stovetop in a large nonstick skillet over medium-low heat for 2 to 3 minutes, stirring frequently. If frozen, thaw in the refrigerator before heating on the stovetop.

PREP TIP: I recommend storing the pico de gallo and Greek yogurt separately so you can easily remove them before reheating. I like to keep a few 2- or 3-ounce containers around that can fit inside a larger container for sauces and toppings I want to keep separate until mealtime.

Calories: 430; Total fat: 20g; Saturated fat: 5g; Sodium: 170mg; Carbohydrates: 41g; Fiber: 9g; Protein: 22g; Calcium: 194mg; Potassium: 936mg

Peach and Feta Farro Salad

PREP TIME: 10 minutes | **COOK TIME**: 40 minutes | **SERVES** 4
REFRIGERATOR: Up to 5 days | **FREEZER:** Not recommended

This cold grain salad has nutty feta to make it feel substantial and is a perfect lunch on the go. The bright, fruity flavors from the peaches and tomatoes will make you forget it's low sodium. It's also always a hit at a hot summer barbecue.

FOR THE FARRO

2 cups whole or semi-pearled farro
6 cups water

1 whole bay leaf

FOR THE SALAD

¼ cup balsamic vinegar
¼ cup olive oil
½ teaspoon Dijon mustard
¼ teaspoon freshly ground black pepper
½ onion, diced

2 Roma tomatoes, diced
2 medium peaches, diced
½ cup crumbled feta
1 to 2 tablespoons chopped
   fresh basil

TO MAKE THE FARRO

1. In a large pot, bring the farro, water, and bay leaf to a boil. Cover, reduce the heat to low, and simmer for 20 to 40 minutes, until tender and chewy and all the liquid has been absorbed. (The cooking time of the farro can vary greatly depending on the type you buy, so be sure to check the package for the suggested cooking time. Whole farro will take the longest to cook.) Remove the bay leaf. Set aside half the farro for the Mini Turkey Meatloaves (page 53).

TO MAKE THE SALAD

2. In a small bowl, whisk the vinegar, olive oil, mustard, and pepper until blended.
3. In a large bowl, mix the farro, tomatoes, peaches, feta, and basil (to taste) and toss in the dressing. Portion equally into 4 containers.

VARIATION: If you can't find farro, you can replace it with another whole grain like brown rice, quinoa, or barley. Prepare the grain according to the package directions.

Calories: 405; Total fat: 18g; Saturated fat: 5g; Sodium: 191mg; Carbohydrates: 53g; Fiber: 10g; Protein: 9g; Calcium: 127mg; Potassium: 481mg

Pork Carnitas Tacos

PREP TIME: 10 minutes | **COOK TIME:** 5 hours | **SERVES** 3 (2 tacos each)
REFRIGERATOR: Up to 5 days | **FREEZER:** Pork can be frozen for up to 6 months

The tender pork filling for these tacos is extremely versatile and can be made ahead and used in many different recipes such as the burrito bowls in this chapter. This recipe uses corn tortillas rather than flour—did you know that corn is a grain, not a vegetable, and whole-kernel corn is a whole grain?

FOR THE PORK

2 pounds boneless pork shoulder, butt, or tenderloin, cut into 2- to 3-inch strips

1 (12-ounce) can no-salt-added diced tomatoes and green chiles

½ onion, diced

½ lime, juiced

2 tablespoons minced garlic

1 teaspoon ground cumin

½ teaspoon cayenne pepper

FOR THE TACOS

6 corn tortillas

3 cups shredded cabbage

1½ cups pico de gallo from Quinoa Scramble (page 45)

TO MAKE THE PORK

1. In a slow cooker or Dutch oven/stockpot, combine the pork, tomatoes and chiles in their juices, onion, lime juice, garlic, cumin, and cayenne pepper.
2. In the slow cooker, cook on low for 5 to 6 hours or on high for 2 to 3 hours until the pork easily shreds with a fork. On the stovetop, cook covered over medium-low heat for 3 to 5 hours. Let the pork cool to room temperature.
3. Set aside half of the pork for the Pork Burrito Bowls (page 52).

TO MAKE THE TACOS

4. Divide the pork among 3 containers with 2 corn tortillas, 1 cup of cabbage, and ½ cup of pico de gallo.

REHEAT: In the microwave, heat the pork on high in 30-second increments until warm. Keep the cabbage and pico de gallo cold.

PREP TIP: I like to use a container with 3 sections for this dish so I can store the pork, the tortillas, and the cabbage and pico de gallo separately. This prevents your tacos from getting soggy. When you are ready to eat, remove and reheat the pork. You can also warm up the tortillas for a few seconds. Then assemble the tacos just like the day they were made.

VARIATION: Try this recipe with 2 pounds of boneless, skinless chicken breast instead of pork and cook until the chicken easily falls apart when shredded with a fork. You can also mix up your toppings. I recommend trying sodium-free options like lettuce, spinach, or avocado.

Calories: 362; Total fat: 7g; Saturated fat: 2g; Sodium: 138mg; Carbohydrates: 36g; Fiber: 7g; Protein: 40g; Calcium: 132mg; Potassium: 1,176mg

Pork Burrito Bowl

PREP TIME: 10 minutes | **SERVES** 3 | **REFRIGERATOR:** Up to 5 days
FREEZER: Pork can be frozen for up to 6 months

Burrito bowls offer an endless variety of possibilities to mix and match ingredients and introduce tons of flavor without salt. This recipe highlights another way to use the carnitas.

Pork set aside from Pork Carnitas Tacos (page 50)
Quinoa and black bean mixture set aside from Quinoa Scramble (page 45)
3 cups shredded cabbage
1½ cups pico de gallo from Quinoa Scramble (page 45)
½ cup plain Greek yogurt
Chopped fresh cilantro, for garnish (optional)

In each of 3 containers, arrange a third of the quinoa and black beans, a third of the pork, 1 cup of shredded cabbage, ½ cup of pico de gallo, and 1 to 2 tablespoons of Greek yogurt. Top with fresh cilantro to taste.

REHEAT: Heat in the microwave on high in 30-second increments until warm or in the oven at 350°F for 5 to 10 minutes.

PREP TIP: Use small containers to keep cold items separate to easily remove them when reheating. I personally don't mind the cabbage heated up, but I keep the pico de gallo and yogurt on the side.

VARIATION: You can make countless varieties of this dish by replacing or adding different components. Try brown rice, pinto beans, chicken, roasted vegetables, brown rice, corn, or different homemade salsas (without the salt!), just to name a few.

Calories: 508; Total fat: 15g; Saturated fat: 4g; Sodium: 145mg; Carbohydrates: 49g; Fiber: 11g; Protein: 47g; Calcium: 194mg; Potassium: 1,635mg

Mini Turkey Meatloaves

PREP TIME: 10 minutes | **COOK TIME:** 25 minutes | **SERVES** 4 (2 mini meatloaves each)
REFRIGERATOR: Up to 5 days | **FREEZER:** Up to 6 months

Baking your mini meatloaf in a muffin tin drastically cuts down on the cooking time and makes it super easy to portion it into individual servings. I like to use oatmeal instead of traditional bread crumbs for a whole-grain twist.

Farro set aside from Peach and Feta
   Farro Salad (page 48)
Nonstick cooking spray
1 pound lean ground turkey
½ cup quick oats
½ onion, finely chopped

1 large egg
2 tablespoons Italian seasoning, divided
2 teaspoons minced garlic
¼ teaspoon freshly ground black pepper
2 or 3 heads broccoli, cut into florets
2 tablespoons olive oil

1. Evenly divide the farro among 4 containers.
2. Preheat the oven to 400°F. Grease a muffin tin with nonstick cooking spray and set aside.
3. In a large bowl, mix the turkey, oats, onion, egg, 1 tablespoon of Italian seasoning, the garlic, and pepper. Separate the mixture into 8 equal pieces and press them into the muffin tin. Bake them in the oven for 18 to 20 minutes.
4. Spread the broccoli on a parchment paper–lined baking sheet and toss with the olive oil and the remaining 1 tablespoon of Italian seasoning. Roast in the oven for 20 minutes.
5. Add a quarter of the broccoli and 2 mini meatloaves to each container on top of the farro.

CONTINUED

REHEAT: In the microwave, heat on high in 30-second intervals, turning and stirring the broccoli and farro in between. You can cut up the meatloaf to help it reheat faster or reheat it separately to avoid overcooking the broccoli and farro. To use the oven, place in an oven-safe dish and heat at 350°F for 5 to 10 minutes.

PREP TIP: You can make these mini meatloaves and freeze them alone. Then you need only reheat them and make the broccoli and farro for a fast and easy dinner at home for you or the entire family.

VARIATION: I chose broccoli and farro for this week, but you can try the mini meatloaves with any vegetable and whole grain. You can also use lean ground beef instead of ground turkey.

Calories: 581; Total fat: 20g; Saturated fat: 4g; Sodium: 205mg; Carbohydrates: 70g; Fiber: 17g; Protein: 38g; Calcium: 204mg; Potassium: 1,451mg

CHAPTER FOUR

Week 3: Focus on Fruits

Personally, I'm tired of fruit getting a bad rap for being high in sugar. Sure, fruits contain natural sugars; however, people with higher fruit and vegetable intake tend to have fewer health problems. A 2021 study in the *Journal of Clinical Endocrinology & Metabolism* found that eating two servings of fruit daily actually reduced the risk of type 2 diabetes by 36 percent.

Fruit is high in healthy antioxidants and fiber, and it offers a sweet and tangy flavor to complement herbs and spices. I chose the theme for this chapter to show you how to use fruit in different ways in sweet and savory dishes.

Recipe List

SHOPPING LIST

Pantry Items

- Almonds, sliced (4 to 5 ounces)
- Baking soda
- Black pepper
- Brown rice (6 ounces)
- Cayenne pepper
- Cinnamon, ground
- Coconut, shredded (8 ounces)
- Curry powder, sodium-free
- Flour, whole-wheat (5 ounces)
- Garlic, minced in oil (1 [16-ounce] container)
- Honey (4 ounces)
- Maple syrup (8 ounces)
- Mayonnaise (8 ounces)
- Mixed vegetables, no-salt-added (1 [15-ounce] can)
- Nuts of choice, unsalted (8 to 10 ounces)
- Oats, quick (5 ounces)
- Olive oil (8 ounces)
- Pineapple, chunks in 100 percent juice (1 [8-ounce] can)
- Ranch dressing, low-sodium (12 ounces)
- Red pepper flakes
- Vegetable oil (8 ounces)

Produce

- Baby carrots (2 pounds)
- Banana (1)
- Broccoli (2 heads)
- Cucumber (1)
- Grapes, seedless (4 to 5 pounds)
- Limes (2)
- Mandarin oranges in 100 percent fruit juice (1 [12-ounce] can)
- Mangoes (2)
- Napa cabbage, shredded (10 ounces)
- Strawberries (1 pound)
- Sweet potato (1)

Meat and Seafood

- Chicken breast, boneless, skinless (1 ½ pounds)
- Mahi-mahi fillets (4) (about 1 pound)

Dairy and Eggs

- Eggs, large (9)
- Greek yogurt, plain (30 ounces)

Be Sure to Have on Hand

- 2 baking sheets or roasting pans
- Chef's knife
- Colander
- Cutting board
- Measuring cups and spoons
- Medium saucepan with lid
- Mixing bowls
- Muffin tin
- Nonstick cooking spray or muffin liners
- Parchment paper
- Slow cooker, large stockpot, or Dutch oven
- Storage containers
  » 21 (20- to 25-ounce) containers including:
    » 3 divided containers with 2 sections
    » 4 divided containers with 4 to 5 sections
    » 4 mason jars
- Whisk

Week 3

	Breakfast	Lunch	Dinner
Day 1	Fruit and Yogurt Parfait	Tropical Chicken Salad	Chili-Lime Mahi-Mahi Sheet Pan Meal
Day 2	Fruit and Yogurt Parfait	Snack Lunch Box	Pineapple Chicken and Rice
Day 3	Fruit and Yogurt Parfait	Tropical Chicken Salad	Chili-Lime Mahi-Mahi Sheet Pan Meal
Day 4	Whole-Wheat Banana Muffins	Tropical Chicken Salad	Chili-Lime Mahi-Mahi Sheet Pan Meal
Day 5	Fruit and Yogurt Parfait	Snack Lunch Box	Pineapple Chicken and Rice
Day 6	Whole-Wheat Banana Muffins	Snack Lunch Box	Chili-Lime Mahi-Mahi Sheet Pan Meal
Day 7	Whole-Wheat Banana Muffins	Snack Lunch Box	Pineapple Chicken and Rice

Step-by-Step Meal Prep

1. Cook the chicken for the Tropical Chicken Salad (page 67) and Pineapple Chicken and Rice (page 69) through step 2.

2. Prepare the marinade for the Chili-Lime Mahi-Mahi Sheet Pan Meal (page 70) and marinate the fish.

3. Preheat the oven to 400°F.

4. Cook the eggs for the Snack Lunch Box (page 66).

5. When the fish is marinated, complete the Chili-Lime Mahi-Mahi Sheet Pan Meal through step 6.

6. Reduce the oven to 350°F and complete the Whole-Wheat Banana Muffins (page 62) through step 3.

7. Cook the rice for Pineapple Chicken and Rice.

8. While the rice cooks, complete the Snack Lunch Box and Fruit and Yogurt Parfait (page 64).

9. Once the rice has finished cooking, complete step 5 of the Pineapple Chicken and Rice recipe.

10. When the chicken is finished and has cooled for 15 minutes, portion it to complete the Tropical Chicken Salad and Pineapple Chicken and Rice recipes.

11. Allow all the items to cool. Portion, pack, label, and store! Freeze two portions of Whole-Wheat Banana Muffins, one portion of Pineapple Chicken and Rice, and one portion of Chili-Lime Mahi-Mahi Sheet Pan Meal.

Whole-Wheat Banana Muffins

PREP TIME: 15 minutes | **COOK TIME:** 25 minutes | **SERVES** 3 (2 muffins each)
REFRIGERATOR: Up to 5 days | **FREEZER:** Up to 6 months

Baking with whole-wheat flour doesn't have to be difficult. Greek yogurt helps keep these muffins extra moist and adds an extra punch of protein to this breakfast staple. I've also added straw-berries on the side because fresh fruit can be a great salt-free addition to any meal.

Nonstick cooking spray (optional)
1 medium ripe banana, mashed
½ cup plain Greek yogurt
¼ cup vegetable oil
3 tablespoons maple syrup
2 tablespoons honey
1 large egg

1 cup whole-wheat flour
1 teaspoon ground cinnamon
½ teaspoon baking soda
2 to 3 tablespoons dry oats, chia seeds, and/or shredded coconut (optional)
1 pound strawberries

1. Preheat the oven to 350°F. Prepare 6 muffin cups of a muffin tin with cooking spray or muffin liners.
2. In a large bowl, combine the banana, yogurt, oil, maple syrup, honey, and egg and mix to form a gooey paste. Slowly stir in the flour, cinnamon, and baking soda.
3. Divide the mixture evenly into the 6 prepared muffin cups. Sprinkle with toppings (if using). Bake for 20 to 25 minutes, until the muffins are golden brown on top and a toothpick inserted into the center comes out clean.
4. Wash and dry the strawberries. Evenly distribute them among 3 divided containers and add 2 muffins to each container.

PREP TIP: Bananas not ripe enough? Put them in a plastic bag for a few hours to overnight to help them ripen faster.

VARIATION: Add ½ cup of unsalted walnuts, but remember this will add about 50 extra calories per serving, mostly from healthy polyunsaturated fatty acids!

Calories: 525; Total fat: 23g; Saturated fat: 3g; Sodium: 258mg; Carbohydrates: 77g; Fiber: 9g; Protein: 10g; Calcium: 128mg; Potassium: 657mg

Fruit and Yogurt Parfait

PREP TIME: 30 minutes | **COOK TIME:** 20 minutes | **SERVES** 4
REFRIGERATOR: Up to 5 days | **FREEZER:** Up to 3 months

This simple yogurt parfait includes three important food groups: fruit, whole grains, and dairy. Greek yogurt is a great source of protein and calcium, whole grains provide fiber, and the mangoes and oranges are good sources of vitamin A. The sweet acidity from the fruit is a perfect accompaniment to the tartness of the yogurt. Adding granola completes this breakfast with a nice crunch.

¼ cup vegetable oil
¼ cup honey
¼ teaspoon ground cinnamon
1½ cups quick oats
½ cup sliced almonds

3 cups vanilla Greek yogurt
2 mangoes, peeled, pitted, and diced
1 (12-ounce) can mandarin oranges in
    100 percent fruit juice, drained

1. Preheat the oven to 350°F. Line a baking sheet with parchment paper. In a large bowl, whisk together the oil, honey, and cinnamon. Add the oats and almonds and toss to coat.
2. Transfer the oat mixture to the baking sheet and press it into an even layer. Bake for 15 to 20 minutes, stirring halfway through, until it appears golden brown and has a sweet, toasted smell. The mixture may still appear wet, but it will dry as it cools. Press down on the granola while it is still warm to form clumps. Allow it to cool completely.
3. In a mason jar, layer about a quarter of the yogurt (about ¾ cup), mangoes, oranges, and granola. Repeat for the remaining 3 mason jars.

PREP TIP: Layer the fruit between the yogurt and granola to prevent the granola from getting soggy. Thaw frozen parfaits in the refrigerator overnight and mix well before eating.

VARIATION: Replace the canned oranges with 1½ cup of peeled and sliced fresh seedless oranges or tangerines. If you want to save time, you can purchase premade granola; aim for a brand that has no sodium and fewer than 10 grams of added sugar. You could also replace the granola with ¼ cup of unsalted toasted nuts or seeds per serving.

Calories: 635; Total fat: 28g; Saturated fat: 6g; Sodium: 91mg; Carbohydrates: 85g; Fiber: 9g; Protein: 17g; Calcium: 303mg; Potassium: 916mg

Snack Lunch Box

PREP TIME: 20 minutes | **COOK TIME:** 15 minutes | **SERVES** 4
REFRIGERATOR: Up to 7 days | **FREEZER:** Not recommended

Relive your childhood with this grown-up upgrade on a school lunch box. Mixing raw fruits and vegetables with hearty proteins provides lasting energy with little sodium! If you are gluten-free, just make sure to check the ingredients of your dressing.

8 large eggs
1 cucumber, cut into ½-inch slices
2 pounds baby carrots

½ cup low-sodium ranch dressing
4 to 5 pounds seedless grapes
1 cup unsalted nuts of your choice

1. Put the eggs in a large saucepan and cover them with water by 1 to 2 inches. Cover and bring to a boil over high heat. Turn off the heat and let the eggs sit in the saucepan for 10 to 12 minutes for a fully hard-boiled egg. If you like your yolks slightly runny, cook for less time. Drain, rinse with cold water, and allow to cool completely.

2. In a 4-compartment container, add a quarter of the cucumber and 10 to 12 baby carrots to one section, 2 tablespoons of ranch dressing to the second section, and 15 grapes and ¼ cup of unsalted nuts in the third section. Leave one section empty for the eggs. Repeat with 3 more containers.

3. Once the eggs have cooled, add 2 eggs to each container. Seal and store in the refrigerator.

VARIATION: You can make endless variations of snack lunch boxes. The goal is to choose 2 to 3 raw fruits or vegetables and 2 to 3 proteins or fats, like unsalted nuts and seeds, hard-boiled eggs, low-sodium dressing, or yogurt.

Calories: 581; Total fat: 41g; Saturated fat: 7g; Sodium: 277mg; Carbohydrates: 36g; Fiber: 9g; Protein: 22g; Calcium: 219mg; Potassium: 955mg

Tropical Chicken Salad

PREP TIME: 15 minutes | **COOK TIME:** 5 hours | **SERVES** 3 | **REFRIGERATOR:** Up to 5 days | **FREEZER:** Up to 6 months

Pineapple adds sweetness and acid to balance the spicy kick from the curry powder in this simple chicken dish. The chicken base for this dish can be eaten many ways. Here, we transform it into a refreshing cold salad.

FOR THE CHICKEN

1½ pounds boneless, skinless
  chicken breast
1 (8-ounce) can crushed
  pineapple, drained

1 tablespoon sodium-free
  curry powder
Juice of ½ lime

FOR THE SALAD

2 tablespoons shredded coconut
2 tablespoons mayonnaise

1 (10-ounce) bag shredded
  napa cabbage

TO MAKE THE CHICKEN

1. In slow cooker, large stockpot, or Dutch oven, combine the chicken breast, pineapple, curry powder, and lime juice. In the slow cooker, cook on low for 5 to 6 hours or on high for 2 to 3 hours, until the chicken shreds easily with a fork. On the stovetop, cook covered over medium-low heat for 3 to 5 hours.
2. Using 2 forks, pull apart the chicken until it is finely shredded and let cool. Set aside half of the shredded chicken for the Pineapple Chicken and Rice (page 69).

CONTINUED

TO MAKE THE SALAD

3. While the chicken is cooking, toast the coconut in a small skillet over medium-low heat. Stir continually for about 5 minutes until the coconut is slightly brown.
4. In a medium bowl, mix half of the cooled chicken and the mayonnaise until well combined.
5. Layer 3 containers with a third of the shredded cabbage, a third of the shredded chicken and mayo mixture, and a third of the toasted coconut.

VARIATION: Replace the napa cabbage with any other type of shredded cabbage or lettuce without changing the sodium or calorie content.

Calories: 262; Total fat: 11g; Saturated fat: 3g; Sodium: 129mg; Carbohydrates: 13g; Fiber: 4g; Protein: 27g; Calcium: 62mg; Potassium: 627mg

Pineapple Chicken and Rice

PREP TIME: 40 minutes | **COOK TIME:** 40 minutes | **SERVES** 3
REFRIGERATOR: Up to 5 days | **FREEZER:** Up to 6 months

Chicken and rice is a one-pot dinner staple in many places around the world. This recipe uses pineapple to add tangy sweetness to the chicken and dresses up simple but nutritious brown rice with some mixed vegetables and big flavor.

1 (15-ounce) can no-salt-added mixed vegetables
1½ cups water
¾ cup brown rice

1 tablespoon minced garlic in olive oil
Juice of ½ lime
Chicken set aside from Tropical Chicken Salad (page 67)

1. Drain the excess liquid from the mixed vegetables in a colander. In a medium saucepan, bring the water to a boil over high heat. Add the rice, garlic, vegetables, and lime juice.
2. Bring to a boil, cover, and reduce the heat to low. Simmer without stirring for 25 to 35 minutes until the rice is tender and all the liquid is absorbed.
3. Remove the rice from the heat and allow to sit covered in the pot for 10 to 20 minutes. Fluff with a fork and divide the rice among 3 containers.
4. Top each with a third of the shredded chicken.

REHEAT: In the microwave, heat on high in 30-second intervals, stirring in between, until the food reaches the desired temperature. To use the oven, place in an oven-safe dish and heat at 350°F for 5 to 10 minutes. If frozen, you can thaw in the refrigerator overnight or heat directly from the freezer.

VARIATION: Replace with any other whole grains and prepare according to the package directions.

Calories: 393; Total fat: 5g; Saturated fat: 1g; Sodium: 91mg; Carbohydrates: 54g; Fiber: 7g; Protein: 32g; Calcium: 68mg; Potassium: 776mg

Chili Lime Mahi-Mahi Sheet Pan Meal

PREP TIME: 40 minutes | **COOK TIME:** 40 minutes | **SERVES** 4
REFRIGERATOR: Up to 5 days | **FREEZER:** Up to 3 months

This easy recipe brings the heat, so you won't miss the salt. Lime is the perfect tangy complement to the spicy red pepper flakes in this simple fish dish.

Juice of 1 lime
3 tablespoons olive oil, divided
1 tablespoon honey
1 tablespoon minced garlic in olive oil
1 teaspoon red pepper flakes
½ teaspoon chili powder or red
  cayenne pepper

4 mahi-mahi or red snapper fillets
  (about 1 pound)
2 broccoli heads, cut into florets
1 large sweet potato, cut into
  ½-inch-wide fries
1 teaspoon freshly ground
  black pepper

1. Preheat the oven to 400°F.
2. In a medium bowl, whisk the lime juice, 2 tablespoons of olive oil, the honey, garlic, red pepper flakes, and chili powder. Add the fish and marinate for at least 30 minutes.
3. While the fish is marinating, spread the broccoli and potatoes on a parchment paper–lined baking sheet and toss with the remaining 1 tablespoon of olive oil and the black pepper.
4. Bake the broccoli and sweet potatoes for 25 to 30 minutes, until the broccoli is slightly brown on the edges and the potatoes easily slip off a fork.
5. Place the fillets on another parchment paper–lined baking sheet and drizzle the marinade over them.
6. Bake the fish for 15 to 18 minutes or until it flakes apart with a fork.
7. Divide the broccoli and potatoes evenly among 4 containers with a fish fillet in each.

REHEAT: In the microwave, reheat in 30-second intervals, rotating the plate in between, until the food reaches the desired temperature. To use the oven, place in an oven-safe dish and heat at 350°F for 5 to 10 minutes. If frozen, you can thaw in the refrigerator overnight or heat directly from the freezer.

VARIATION: Substitute any other type of 4-ounce white fish fillets for the mahi-mahi or any type of potatoes for the sweet potatoes. Directions and cooking times remain the same.

Calories: 356; Total fat: 13g; Saturated fat: 2g; Sodium: 192mg; Carbohydrates: 33g; Fiber: 9g; Protein: 32g; Calcium: 195mg; Potassium: 1,567mg

CHAPTER FIVE

Week 4: Beans— They're Good for Your Heart!

You may remember the silly rhyme from when you were a kid, but science supports it. Soluble fiber found in beans helps bind cholesterol in the GI tract and lower LDL cholesterol.

Although fiber is beneficial, suddenly increasing your fiber intake may cause some discomfort in the form of bloating, gas, and loose stools. The recipes in this book have been designed so that you will have been slowly increasing your fiber intake to this point to avoid any discomfort. If you haven't been following the previous recipes or have a sensitive stomach, limit beans to one meal per day.

Recipe List

Black Bean and Sweet Potato Hash 78

No-Bake Breakfast Cookies 80

White Bean Salsa 81

Bean and Burger Stuffed Peppers 82

Turkey and Edamame Stir-Fry 84

Spicy Chickpea Curry 85

SHOPPING LIST

Pantry Items

- Black beans, no-salt-added (2 [15-ounce] cans)

- Cannellini beans, no-salt-added (1 [15-ounce] can)

- Chickpeas, no-salt-added (1 [15-ounce] can)

- Black pepper

- Brown rice (20 ounces)

- Chia seeds (8 to 10 ounces)

- Coconut milk, full-fat (1 [15-ounce] can)

- Coconut, shredded (8 ounces)

- Cornstarch

- Cumin, ground

- Curry powder, sodium-free

- Garlic, minced in oil (1 [16-ounce] container)

- Honey (4 ounces)

- Italian seasoning

- Ketchup, low-sodium (8 ounces)

- Oats, quick (3 ounces)

- Olive oil (8 ounces)

- Peanut butter, creamy, no-salt-added (1 jar)

- Red wine vinegar (8 ounces)

- Soy sauce, low-sodium (4 ounces)

- Tomatoes, diced, no-salt-added (1 [15-ounce] can)

- Tomatoes with green chiles, diced, no-salt-added (1 [12-ounce] can)

- Tortilla chips, low-sodium (1 [10- to 15-ounce] bag)

- Vanilla extract (2 ounces)

- Walnuts, unsalted (4 ounces)

Produce

- Apples or oranges (3)

- Banana peppers (4)

- Bell peppers, red (2)

- Bell peppers, yellow or orange (4)

- Jalapeño pepper (1)

- Onions (2)

- Parsley, fresh (1 bunch)

- Spinach, baby (5 ounces)

- Sweet potatoes (2)

- Tomatoes, Roma (2)

Meat and Seafood

- Turkey, lean ground (1 pound)

Dairy and Eggs

- Jack cheese, shredded (9 ounces)

Frozen

- Edamame, shelled (1 [16-ounce]
  bag or 1 [16-ounce] can),
  no-salt-added

Be Sure to Have on Hand

- Baking sheets or
  roasting pans

- Chef's knife

- Colander

- Cutting board

- Large frying pan lid

- Large saucepan with lid

- Measuring cups and spoons

- Mixing bowls: 2 small and 2 medium
  to large

- Storage containers
  » 21 (20- to 25-ounce) containers
    including:
    » 6 divided containers with
      2 sections

- Whisk

Week 4

	Breakfast	Lunch	Dinner
Day 1	Black Bean and Sweet Potato Hash	White Bean Salsa	Spicy Chickpea Curry
Day 2	No-Bake Breakfast Cookies	Bean and Burger Stuffed Peppers	Turkey and Edamame Stir-Fry
Day 3	Black Bean and Sweet Potato Hash	Bean and Burger Stuffed Peppers	Spicy Chickpea Curry
Day 4	No-Bake Breakfast Cookies	White Bean Salsa	Turkey and Edamame Stir-Fry
Day 5	Black Bean and Sweet Potato Hash	Bean and Burger Stuffed Peppers	Spicy Chickpea Curry
Day 6	No-Bake Breakfast Cookies	Bean and Burger Stuffed Peppers	Turkey and Edamame Stir-Fry
Day 7	Black Bean and Sweet Potato Hash	White Bean Salsa	Spicy Chickpea Curry

Step-by-Step Meal Prep

1. Start by making the rice for the Bean and Burger Stuffed Peppers (page 82), Turkey and Edamame Stir-Fry (page 84), and Spicy Chickpea Curry (page 85). Continue making the Spicy Chickpea Curry through step 3.

2. While the rice is cooking, continue with the Bean and Burger Stuffed Peppers and the Turkey and Soybean Stir-Fry through step 8.

3. Once the meat has cooked, set aside half, and complete the Turkey and Edamame Stir-Fry.

4. Preheat the oven to 325°F and complete the Bean and Burger Stuffed Peppers.

5. While the peppers bake, complete the Spicy Chickpea Curry (page 85) and Black Bean and Sweet Potato Hash (page 78).

6. While everything is cooling, make the No-Bake Breakfast Cookies (page 80) and White Bean Salsa (page 81).

7. Once everything is cool, portion, pack, label, and store! Freeze one portion of Black Bean and Sweet Potato Hash, one portion of Bean and Burger Stuffed Peppers, one portion of White Bean Salsa, one portion of Spicy Chickpea Curry, and one portion of Turkey and Edamame Stir-Fry.

Black Bean and Sweet Potato Hash

PREP TIME: 20 minutes | **COOK TIME:** 25 minutes | **SERVES** 4
REFRIGERATOR: Up to 5 days | **FREEZER:** Up to 6 months

Black beans are one of the most used beans because of their versatility. This breakfast dish demonstrates how to incorporate these protein-packed powerhouses to provide you with energy all morning.

2 medium sweet potatoes, cut into
  ½-inch chunks
1 tablespoon olive oil
½ white onion, chopped
1 red bell pepper, chopped
1 teaspoon minced garlic
  in olive oil

1 (15-ounce) can no-salt-added black
  beans, drained and rinsed
2 Roma tomatoes, chopped
½ teaspoon sodium-free Italian
  seasoning
¼ teaspoon ground cumin
5 ounces fresh baby spinach

1. Put the sweet potatoes in a medium saucepan and cover with water by about 1½ inches. Bring to a boil over medium-high heat and simmer for about 8 minutes until the potatoes are tender. Drain and set aside.
2. Heat the olive oil in a large saucepan over medium-high heat, and sauté the onion, bell pepper, and garlic until tender, 6 to 7 minutes. Add the potatoes, black beans, tomatoes, Italian seasoning, and cumin. Reduce the heat to medium and cook for 5 to 10 minutes, until the excess liquid is mostly gone and the potatoes are slightly browned.
3. While the hash is simmering, divide the spinach among 4 containers.
4. Once the hash finishes cooking, allow it to cool for 5 to 10 minutes before topping the spinach in each container with a quarter of the mixture.

REHEAT: Reheat in the microwave on high, partially covered, in 30-second increments. Stir in between. Warm up on the stovetop over medium heat for 3 to 4 minutes or until the food reaches the desired temperature.

PREP TIP: Don't stir the potatoes too often or they will break apart and not get brown.

VARIATION: Sensitive stomach or can't find the beans? Replace the black beans with about a cup of chopped low-sodium ham (which will make the recipe no longer vegan).

Calories: 206; Total fat: 4g; Saturated fat: 1g; Sodium: 70mg; Carbohydrates: 35g; Fiber: 10g; Protein: 9g; Calcium: 86mg; Potassium: 880mg

No-Bake Breakfast Cookies

PREP TIME: 10 minutes | **COOK TIME**: 5 minutes | **SERVES** 3 (3 cookies each)
REFRIGERATOR: Up to 7 days | **FREEZER:** Up to 6 months

Did you know that peanuts are technically legumes? Nutritionally we treat them more like nuts because they do not contain as many carbs as other legumes, but they do have unsaturated fats and many healthy nutrients, including magnesium.

¾ cup no-salt-added creamy
   peanut butter
2 tablespoons honey
1 teaspoon vanilla extract
¾ cup quick oats

1 tablespoon chia seeds
1 tablespoon shredded coconut
2 tablespoons chopped walnuts
3 medium apples or oranges

1. In a medium microwave-safe bowl, combine the peanut butter, honey, and vanilla. Microwave for 20 seconds to soften and stir together.
2. Add the oats, chia seeds, coconut, and walnuts and combine well. Divide the mixture into 9 identical balls and lightly press them to flatten.
3. Place the balls on a baking sheet in the freezer for 30 to 60 minutes, until hard. Then transfer 3 cookies into 3 individual containers.
4. Enjoy with a medium piece of fruit.

VARIATION: Try mixing in different types of unsalted seeds, nuts, and dried fruits, but be careful of added sugar when choosing ingredients.

Calories: 659; Total fat: 39g; Saturated fat: 7g; Sodium: 16mg; Carbohydrates: 67g; Fiber: 12g; Protein: 19g; Calcium: 89mg; Potassium: 678mg

White Bean Salsa

PREP TIME: 15 minutes | **SERVES** 3 | **REFRIGERATOR:** Up to 5 days | **FREEZER:** Up to 6 months

Is it a salad? A dip? This white bean salsa is a great accompaniment to any meal but also can be a meal in itself. Cannellini beans provide a savory umami flavor to this refreshing cold dish.

1 (15-ounce) can no-salt-added cannellini beans, drained and rinsed
2 tablespoons red wine vinegar
1 tablespoon olive oil
¼ teaspoon ground cumin
¼ teaspoon freshly ground black pepper

1 (12-ounce) can no-salt-added diced tomatoes and green chiles, drained
1 red bell pepper, chopped
½ white onion, chopped
3 cups unsalted tortilla chips

1. Lay a dry paper towel or cloth on a clean cutting board. Spread the beans on the towel to dry for 5 to 10 minutes.
2. In a large bowl, whisk the vinegar, olive oil, cumin, and black pepper. Add the beans, tomatoes and green chiles, bell pepper, and onion, and mix until coated well with the dressing.
3. Divide evenly into 3 separate containers with 1 cup of chips each.

PREP TIP: Use a container with 2 compartments to keep the chips from becoming soggy.

VARIATION: Try this salad with any sodium-free beans of your choice. Sensitive to beans? Substitute sodium-free whole-kernel sweet corn.

Calories: 323; Total fat: 11g; Saturated fat: 1g; Sodium: 20mg; Carbohydrates: 45g; Fiber: 10g; Protein: 11g; Calcium: 123mg; Potassium: 748mg

Bean and Burger Stuffed Peppers

PREP TIME: 45 minutes | **COOK TIME:** 1 hour | **SERVES** 4 | **REFRIGERATOR:** Up to 5 days | **FREEZER:** Up to 6 months

Stuffed peppers have always been a classic make-ahead meal in my house. My mom would cook a batch and freeze them for months to have an easy pre-prepped lunch or dinner option.

FOR THE RICE

6 cups water
3 cups brown rice

½ tablespoon olive oil

FOR THE TURKEY

1 pound lean ground turkey
½ white onion, chopped
1 tablespoon minced garlic in olive oil

1 tablespoon low-sodium soy sauce
1 teaspoon ground cumin
½ teaspoon freshly ground black pepper

FOR THE STUFFED PEPPERS

4 yellow or orange bell peppers, seeded and halved
1 (15-ounce) can no-salt-added black beans, drained and rinsed

¼ cup low-sodium ketchup
1½ cups shredded Jack cheese
1 to 2 tablespoons chopped fresh cilantro

TO MAKE THE RICE

1. In a medium saucepan, bring the water to a boil over high heat. Add the rice and olive oil.
2. Bring the water back to a boil, cover, and reduce the heat to low. Cook without stirring for 25 to 35 minutes until the rice is tender and all the liquid is absorbed.
3. Remove from heat and allow to sit covered in the pot for 10 to 20 minutes. Fluff with a fork. Set aside a third of the cooked rice for the Turkey and Edamame Stir-Fry (Page 84) and another third for the Spicy Chickpea Curry (page 85). Measure out 1 cup from the remaining third and set aside the rest for this recipe.

TO MAKE THE TURKEY

4. Place a large skillet over medium-high heat and brown the turkey, breaking it apart with the spatula. Continue to stir the meat frequently so it cooks evenly.
5. Halfway through the meat browning, about 7 minutes, add the onions and continue to cook until the meat is cooked through, about 15 minutes. Drain and discard any excess fat from the pan.
6. Add the garlic, soy sauce, cumin, and black pepper. Divide and set aside half for the Turkey and Edamame Stir-Fry (page 84).

TO MAKE THE STUFFED PEPPERS

7. Preheat the oven to 325°F.
8. Place the peppers, cut-side up, on a baking sheet.
9. In a large bowl, mix the 1 cup of reserved rice, the turkey mixture, the black beans, and the ketchup. Scoop the mixture into the bell peppers and top with the shredded cheese.
10. Bake for 20 to 25 minutes until the cheese is melted and slightly brown.
11. Remove and let the peppers cool for 10 to 15 minutes. Fill 4 containers with 2 halves each. Top each serving with 1 to 2 teaspoons of cilantro.

REHEAT: Heat in the microwave for 1 minute on 70 percent power. Continue in 20-second increments until heated through. In the oven, heat at 350°F for 8 to 10 minutes.

VARIATION: Try this recipe with diced mushrooms instead of black beans. Replace the black beans with 1 pint of white button mushrooms. Chop the mushrooms and add them to the pan with the onions. If you like spice, try adding sliced jalapeño along with the cilantro.

Calories: 577; Total fat: 20g; Saturated fat: 10g; Sodium: 368mg; Carbohydrates: 69g; Fiber: 9g; Protein: 22g; Calcium: 392mg; Potassium: 979mg

Turkey and Edamame Stir-Fry

PREP TIME: 10 minutes | **COOK TIME:** 5 minutes | **SERVES** 3
REFRIGERATOR: Up to 5 days | **FREEZER:** Up to 6 months

Edamame are whole soybeans, and they have many nutritional benefits. Adding edamame to this stir-fry help make it more satisfying by
increasing the fiber, protein, and healthy fat content. Stir-fries make
great meal prep because they are quick and often better a day or
two later when the flavors have had time to meld.

Rice set aside from Bean and Burger
   Stuffed Peppers (page 82)
Turkey mixture set aside from Bean and
   Burger Stuffed Peppers (page 82)

16 ounces shelled edamame, frozen
   and defrosted or canned with
   no salt added

1. Evenly divide the rice among 3 containers and set aside.
2. Place the turkey in a large skillet over medium heat and add the
   edamame. Sauté for 5 minutes and top the rice with the mixture.

REHEAT: In the microwave, heat on high for 1 minute. Stir, then continue to
heat in 30-second increments until heated completely. You can also reheat
on the stovetop over medium heat for 3 to 4 minutes.

VARIATION: Use a can of no-salt-added green beans, drained and rinsed, or
1½ cups of frozen green beans in place of the edamame. Thaw and drain
excess fluid from the frozen beans before adding them in step 2.

Calories: 541; Total fat: 17g; Saturated fat: 3g; Sodium: 150mg;
Carbohydrates: 65g; Fiber: 10g; Protein: 36g; Calcium: 141mg;
Potassium: 1,021mg

Spicy Chickpea Curry

PREP TIME: 30 minutes | **COOK TIME:** 10 minutes | **SERVES** 4
REFRIGERATOR: Up to 5 days | **FREEZER:** Up to 3 months

This dish is inspired by my time living in the US Virgin Islands and the vibrant flavors of the local curries. Many individuals in this region follow vegan diets, and chickpeas are a popular legume easy to find anywhere.

Rice set aside from Bean and Burger Stuffed Peppers (page 82)
1 teaspoon olive oil
½ onion, diced
1 medium jalapeño pepper, diced
4 banana peppers
1 (15-ounce) can no-salt-added chickpeas, drained and rinsed
1 (15-ounce) can no-salt-added diced tomatoes, drained
1½ tablespoons sodium-free curry powder
3 tablespoons water
1½ teaspoons cornstarch
1 (15-ounce) can full-fat coconut milk

1. Divide the rice among 4 storage containers.
2. Heat the olive oil in a large skillet over medium heat and sauté the onions, jalapeño, and banana peppers until lightly caramelized, about 5 minutes.
3. Add the chickpeas, tomatoes, and curry powder. Cook for 1 to 2 minutes.
4. In a small bowl, mix the water and cornstarch until smooth and add this slurry to the skillet along with the coconut milk. Cover, bring to a boil, reduce the heat to low, and simmer for 2 to 3 minutes.
5. Remove the curry from the heat and allow to cool for 10 to 15 minutes. Evenly divide the curry among the 4 containers with the rice.

REHEAT: Heat in the microwave for 1 minute. Stir, then continue to heat in 30-second increments until heated completely. You can also reheat on the stovetop over medium heat for 3 to 4 minutes.

CONTINUED

VARIATION: Replace the beans with 2 boneless, skinless chicken breasts cut into cubes. Add the chicken to the skillet with the onions to allow it more time to cook. Make sure the chicken is cooked through before removing from heat.

Calories: 551; Total fat: 28g; Saturated fat: 21g; Sodium: 36mg; Carbohydrates: 68g; Fiber: 11g; Protein: 13g; Calcium: 126mg; Potassium: 964mg

CHAPTER SIX

Week 5: Fun with Flavor

No one enjoys eating bland, flavorless food. Food is meant to be savored, and just because you can't add salt doesn't mean you can't enjoy different flavors. Experimenting with sweet, acidic, sour, bitter, spicy, and savory tastes can create excitement and complexity in recipes without the need for extra salt. Include elements in your recipes that hit at least two of these flavors to provide depth. You can also play around with combining different textures. Competing textures make it more exciting for our mouths to eat. In this chapter, I wanted to focus on dishes that highlight different flavor and texture combinations.

Recipe List

SHOPPING LIST

Pantry Items

- Balsamic vinegar (8 ounces)

- Bananas, dried (8 ounces)

- Bay leaf, whole (1)

- Black pepper

- Blueberries, dried (8 ounces)

- Cereal, whole-grain (8 ounces)

- Chickpeas, no-salt-added (1 [15-ounce] can)

- Chili powder

- Cinnamon, ground

- Dijon mustard (8 ounces)

- Garlic, minced in oil (1 [16-ounce] container)

- Ginger, ground

- Honey (8 ounces)

- Maple syrup (8 ounces)

- Mixed nuts, unsalted (8 ounces)

- Oats, quick (5 ounces)

- Olive oil (8 ounces)

- Orzo (12 ounces)

- Quinoa (7 ounces)

- Pesto (1 jar)

- Red wine vinegar (8 ounces)

- Salsa, low-sodium (8 ounces)

- Tortillas, corn (10)

- Turmeric, ground

- Vanilla extract (2 ounces)

Produce

- Bell pepper, red (1)

- Carrot (1)

- Celery stalks (2)

- Cucumber (1)

- Jalapeño pepper (1)

- Lemon (1)

- Onion, red (1)

- Onion, white (1)

- Parsley, fresh (1 bunch)
- Snap peas (2 pounds)

- Spinach, baby (5 ounces)

Meat and Seafood

- Chicken breast, boneless, skinless (4) (about 1 pound)

- Pork chops, boneless (3)

Dairy and Eggs

- Milk, low-fat (½ gallon)

- Monterey Jack cheese, shredded (6 ounces)

Be Sure to Have on Hand

- 2 baking sheets or roasting pans
- 2-quart casserole dish
- Chef's knife
- Colander
- Cutting board
- Large stockpot or Dutch oven
- Measuring cups and spoons

- Medium saucepan with lid
- Mixing bowls: 2 small and 2 medium to large
- Storage containers
  » 21 (20- to 25-ounce) containers including:
    » 4 mason jars
- Whisk

Week 5

	Breakfast	Lunch	Dinner
Day 1	Turmeric Oatmeal	Lemon Herb Quinoa Salad	Spicy Chicken Taco Casserole
Day 2	Sunrise Trail Mix	Lemon Herb Quinoa Salad	Spicy Chicken Taco Casserole
Day 3	Turmeric Oatmeal	Chicken Pesto Soup	Honey Balsamic Pork Chops
Day 4	Sunrise Trail Mix	Lemon Herb Quinoa Salad	Spicy Chicken Taco Casserole
Day 5	Turmeric Oatmeal	Chicken Pesto Soup	Honey Balsamic Pork Chops
Day 6	Sunrise Trail Mix	Chicken Pesto Soup	Spicy Chicken Taco Casserole
Day 7	Sunrise Trail Mix	Chicken Pesto Soup	Honey Balsamic Pork Chops

Step-by-Step Meal Prep

1. Preheat the oven to 400°F. Make the Honey Balsamic Pork Chops (page 100) through step 5.

2. While the pork chops are baking, start the Chicken Pesto Soup (page 96) through step 3.

3. Once the chicken is cooked through, complete the Chicken Pesto Soup. When the pork chops finish baking, reduce the heat to 325°F; then complete the Spicy Chicken Taco Casserole (page 102) through step 5.

4. Once the quinoa is cooked and cooled, complete the Lemon Herb Quinoa Salad (page 98) and Honey Balsamic Pork Chops.

5. Make the Sunrise Trail Mix (page 95) through step 2. While the trail mix cooks and cools, make the Turmeric Oatmeal (page 94). Then complete the trail mix.

6. Allow the containers to cool; then label and store! Freeze two portions of Chicken Pesto Soup, one portion of Spicy Chicken Taco Casserole, and one portion of Honey Balsamic Pork Chops.

Turmeric Oatmeal

PREP TIME: 15 minutes | **COOK TIME:** 10 minutes | **SERVES** 3
REFRIGERATOR: Up to 5 days | **FREEZER:** Up to 6 months

Turmeric certainly isn't the first thing that comes to mind when I think of breakfast. But this powerful antioxidant makes a great addition to oatmeal, providing an earthy depth that pairs well with the cinnamon and maple syrup.

3 cups low-fat milk
2 tablespoons maple syrup
1 teaspoon ground turmeric
1 teaspoon ground cinnamon

½ teaspoon ground ginger
½ teaspoon vanilla extract
1½ cups quick oats

1. In a large saucepan over medium heat, combine the milk, maple syrup, turmeric, cinnamon, ginger, and vanilla, and bring to a boil.
2. Add the oats and reduce heat to low. Simmer for 5 to 7 minutes until the oats thicken to your desired consistency. Remember, the oats will continue to thicken some as they cool.
3. Remove the oats from the heat and let cool for 5 to 10 minutes before dividing evenly among 3 containers. Allow to cool completely before storing.

REHEAT: In the microwave, heat on high in 30-second increments, stirring in between, until heated through.

PREP TIP: Be careful with ground turmeric; aside from its flavor, its color is also intense and will easily stain white countertops and your fingers.

VARIATION: Add texture with 1 to 2 tablespoons of toppings like unsalted nuts, chia seeds, or dried fruit left over from other recipes. Make this dish vegan and dairy-free by substituting your favorite milk alternative.

Calories: 268; Total fat: 7g; Saturated fat: 3g; Sodium: 118mg; Carbohydrates: 41g; Fiber: 4g; Protein: 12g; Calcium: 331mg; Potassium: 497mg

Sunrise Trail Mix

PREP TIME: 20 minutes | **COOK TIME:** 15 minutes | **SERVES** 4

REFRIGERATOR: Not required; store in an airtight container at room temperature for up to 30 days | **FREEZER:** Not recommended

Keep your taste buds on their toes by mixing crunchy cereal and nuts with chewy dried blueberries and crispy bananas. Tossing your cereal and nuts in maple syrup and toasting them adds a new dimension of earthy sweetness.

Nonstick cooking spray (optional)
2 tablespoons maple syrup
½ teaspoon ground cinnamon
½ teaspoon vanilla extract
3 cups Cheerios

1 cup unsalted mixed nuts
½ cup dried blueberries
½ cup dried bananas
4 cups low-fat milk

1. Preheat the oven to 325°F. Line a baking sheet with parchment paper or grease it with nonstick cooking spray.
2. In a large bowl, mix the maple syrup, cinnamon, and vanilla. Add the cereal and nuts and toss until they are evenly covered with syrup.
3. Spread the cereal mixture on the baking sheet and toast for 10 to 15 minutes until slightly browned.
4. Remove the mix from the oven and allow to cool for 10 to 15 minutes. Add the dried blueberries and bananas and toss to combine. Separate the trail mix into 4 containers.
5. When ready to eat, mix 1 portion of trail mix in a bowl with 1 cup of low-fat milk.

PREP TIP: Use plain Cheerios without any sugar added. Buy dried bananas without anything added to them, not banana chips.

VARIATION: Replace dried blueberries and bananas with a cup of any dried fruit you like; just make sure it doesn't have any sugar added to it!

Calories: 533; Total fat: 23g; Saturated fat: 7g; Sodium: 227mg; Carbohydrates: 72g; Fiber: 6g; Protein: 17g; Calcium: 412mg; Potassium: 922mg

Chicken Pesto Soup

PREP TIME: 30 minutes | **COOK TIME:** 20 minutes | **SERVES** 4
REFRIGERATOR: Up to 5 days | **FREEZER:** Up to 6 months

Pesto is a sauce that mixes spicy, savory, sweet, and bitter flavors all in one. It is traditionally made using fresh basil, olive oil, garlic, pine nuts, and Parmesan cheese. Pesto often contains salt as well, but when it comes to this tasty condiment, a little goes a long way. Pesto can be used in a variety of recipes from roasted fish to pasta.

4 boneless, skinless chicken breasts (about 1 pound)
8 cups water
1 white onion, peeled and cut into eighths
1 large carrot, cut into 1-inch chunks

2 celery stalks, cut into 1-inch chunks
1 whole bay leaf
4 cups fresh baby spinach
1½ cups uncooked orzo
¼ cup store-bought or homemade pesto sauce

1. In a large stockpot over high heat, combine the chicken, water, onion, carrot, celery, and bay leaf. Bring to a boil, reduce the heat, partially cover, and simmer 10 to 15 minutes, until the chicken is no longer pink in the center, or use a meat thermometer and cook to 165°F.
2. Remove the pot from the heat and transfer the chicken to a cutting board or baking sheet. Allow it to cool for 5 to 10 minutes.
3. Use a slotted spoon to discard the vegetables and bay leaf or strain the broth through a colander lined with a paper towel. Measure 4 cups of the broth and return it to the stockpot.
4. Use 2 forks to shred the chicken. Return half of the chicken to the stockpot and set aside the other half for the Spicy Chicken Taco Casserole (page 102).

5. Add the shredded chicken, spinach, and orzo to the pot and cook over medium-high heat until it boils. Reduce the heat and simmer until the orzo is tender, about 7 minutes.
6. Remove from heat and cool for at least 10 to 15 minutes before dividing into 4 mason jars to finish cooling. Top with the pesto.

REHEAT: Reheat in the microwave for 1 to 2 minutes on high and then in 30-second increments, stirring in between, until the food reaches your desired temperature.

PREP TIP: Look for premade pesto with the lowest amount of sodium per serving. You can also make your own sodium-free pesto by mixing ½ cup of olive oil, 3 garlic cloves, 2 cups of fresh basil, 2 tablespoons of pine nuts, ½ cup of Parmesan cheese, and ¼ teaspoon of freshly ground black pepper in a food processor.

Calories: 322; Total fat: 11g; Saturated fat: 2g; Sodium: 212mg; Carbohydrates: 36g; Fiber: 3g; Protein: 21g; Calcium: 96mg; Potassium: 593mg

Lemon Herb Quinoa Salad

PREP TIME: 15 minutes | **COOK TIME:** 15 minutes | **SERVES** 3
REFRIGERATOR: Up to 5 days | **FREEZER:** Not recommended

Lemon and herbs make a sour and savory combination in the home-made dressing for this bright and refreshing salad. To create more interest in the mouth, I've mixed the soft texture of the quinoa and beans with crunchy raw vegetables.

FOR THE QUINOA

1 cup quinoa, rinsed   **2 cups water**

FOR THE SALAD

Juice of ½ lemon
2 tablespoons olive oil
1 tablespoon red wine vinegar
2 teaspoons minced garlic in olive oil
¼ teaspoon freshly ground black pepper
1 (15-ounce) can no-salt-added
   chickpeas, drained and rinsed

½ red bell pepper, diced
½ red onion, diced
1 cucumber, diced
½ cup chopped fresh parsley

TO MAKE THE QUINOA

1. In a large saucepot over high heat, combine the quinoa and water. Bring to a boil, cover, and reduce the heat to medium-low. Simmer undisturbed for 15 minutes or until all the liquid has been absorbed. Remove the quinoa from the heat and let cool for 5 to 10 minutes. Measure out half of the cooked quinoa and set aside the rest for the Honey Balsamic Pork Chops (page 100).

TO MAKE THE SALAD

2. In a small bowl, whisk together the lemon juice, olive oil, vinegar, garlic, and black pepper.
3. In a large bowl, toss the quinoa, chickpeas, bell pepper, onion, cucumber, parsley, and dressing. Mix until everything is evenly coated and separate into 3 individual containers.

VARIATION: Replace the quinoa with 1 cup of any cooked whole grain of your choice. Try brown rice, farro, barley, or whole-kernel corn.

Calories: 356; Total fat: 13g; Saturated fat: 2g; Sodium: 17mg; Carbohydrates: 49g; Fiber: 10g; Protein: 13g; Calcium: 93mg; Potassium: 687mg

Honey Balsamic Pork Chops

PREP TIME: 20 minutes | **COOK TIME:** 25 minutes | **SERVES** 3
REFRIGERATOR: Up to 5 days | **FREEZER:** Up to 6 months

Sweet honey balances the intense bitter and acidic flavor of the balsamic vinegar while providing a syrupy texture in this savory pork-chop recipe. The combination of flavors will make you forget all about salt.

Quinoa set aside from Lemon Herb
  Quinoa Salad (page 98)
Nonstick cooking spray (optional)
3 pork chops
2 pounds snap peas
1 tablespoon olive oil

½ teaspoon freshly ground black pepper,
  divided
2 tablespoons honey
2 teaspoons balsamic vinegar
2 teaspoons Dijon mustard

1. Divide the quinoa among 3 storage containers.
2. Preheat the oven to 400°F. Line a baking sheet with parchment paper or spray with nonstick cooking spray. Place the pork chops on the baking sheet.
3. In a medium bowl, toss the snap peas, olive oil, and ¼ teaspoon of pepper and spread them on the baking sheet around the pork chops.
4. In a small bowl, whisk the honey, vinegar, mustard, and remaining ¼ teaspoon of pepper. Set aside 2 tablespoons of the mixture.
5. Drizzle or use a pastry brush to evenly distribute the reserved mixture on the pork chops.
6. Cook for 18 to 22 minutes or until the pork is no longer pink and the snap peas are browned and tender.
7. Remove the baking sheet from the oven and top with the reserved honey and vinegar mixture. Allow to cool; then add 1 pork chop and a third of the snap peas to each of the 3 containers on top of the quinoa.

REHEAT: In the microwave, cover the pork with a damp paper towel. Heat at 50 percent power in 1-minute increments. In between, flip and rotate the pork chop and stir the peas and the quinoa. In an oven, heat for 10 to 15 minutes at 350°F.

VARIATION: Replace the snap peas with broccoli or thinly sliced zucchini without changing the cooking time.

Calories: 605; Total fat: 20g; Saturated fat: 5g; Sodium: 141mg; Carbohydrates: 53g; Fiber: 10g; Protein: 52g; Calcium: 160mg; Potassium: 1,471mg

Spicy Chicken Taco Casserole

PREP TIME: 30 minutes | **COOK TIME:** 25 minutes | **SERVES** 4
REFRIGERATOR: Up to 5 days | **FREEZER:** Up to 6 months

Spice may not be for everyone, but it sure can make you forget about salt—fast. This recipe incorporates varying intensities of heat from the salsa, jalapeño, and chili powder.

Nonstick cooking spray
Shredded chicken set aside from
　Chicken Pesto Soup (page 96)
¼ teaspoon red chili powder
　or cayenne pepper
10 corn tortillas

½ cup low-sodium salsa
5 ounces fresh baby spinach
1 medium jalapeño pepper, diced
½ red onion, diced
1 cup of shredded Monterey
　jack cheese

1. Preheat the oven to 325°F. Spray a 2-quart casserole dish with nonstick cooking spray.
2. Sprinkle the chicken with the chili powder.
3. Layer 5 corn tortillas in the bottom of the prepared casserole dish. (If needed, cut the tortillas in halves and quarters to cover the bottom.)
4. Top the tortilla layer with half of the chicken, salsa, spinach, jalapeño, and red onion. Cover with half of the cheese. Repeat with another layer of corn tortillas and the other half of the ingredients.
5. Bake for 20 to 25 minutes, until the cheese is melted and slightly brown.
6. Remove and allow to cool before portioning into 4 containers.

REHEAT: Microwave at 50 percent power in 1-minute increments. In the oven, heat at 350°F for 10 to 15 minutes.

VARIATION: If you don't care for spicy food, leave out the chili powder and even the jalapeño pepper, depending how much heat you can stand.

Calories: 339; Total fat: 12g; Saturated fat: 6g; Sodium: 232mg; Carbohydrates: 35g; Fiber: 12g; Protein: 25g; Calcium: 369mg; Potassium: 481mg

CHAPTER SEVEN

Week 6: The Mediterranean Diet

A Mediterranean diet is not a typical "diet." This way of eating does not restrict any one food or food group but instead promotes a dietary style that limits highly processed foods and puts an emphasis on fresh, seasonal, and local ingredients. More and more research suggests that a Mediterranean diet is related to a lower risk of obesity, diabetes, heart disease, and cancer.

This chapter brings together staples of the Mediterranean diet such as heart-healthy fats, whole grains, fruits, vegetables, and other plant foods like beans and nuts.

Recipe List

SHOPPING LIST

Pantry Items

- Balsamic vinegar (8 ounces)

- Black pepper

- Chickpeas, no-salt-added (1 [15-ounce] can)

- Cumin, ground

- Dijon mustard (8 ounces)

- Garlic, minced in oil (1 [16-ounce] container)

- Honey (4 ounces)

- Italian seasoning, sodium-free

- Kalamata olives, pitted (8 ounces)

- Olive oil (8 ounces)

- Pasta, whole-wheat (½ pound)

- Peanut butter, creamy, no-salt-added (1 jar)

- Pretzels, low-sodium (8 ounces)

- Red pepper flakes

- Red wine vinegar (8 ounces)

- Vanilla extract (2 ounces)

- Waffles, whole-wheat, frozen (box of 6)

- Wine, dry white (1 [750 ml] bottle)

Produce

- Baby carrots (1 pound)

- Bell pepper, red (1)

- Cucumbers (2)

- Grapes, seedless (2 pounds)

- Green beans (1 pound)

- Jalapeño pepper (1)

- Lemon (1)

- Red onion (1)

- Red potatoes (8)

- Rosemary, fresh (1 bunch)

- Spinach, baby (12 ounces)

- Tomatoes, Roma or plum (2)

Meat and Seafood

- Chicken thighs (4) (about 1½ pounds)

Dairy and Eggs

- Cheddar cheese, shredded (6 ounces)

- Eggs, large (12)

- Feta cheese, crumbled (6 ounces)

- Greek yogurt, plain (20 ounces)

- Parmesan cheese, grated (2 ounces)

Be Sure to Have on Hand

- 2 medium saucepans, one with a lid

- Baking sheet or roasting pan

- Chef's knife

- Colander

- Cutting board

- Food processor, blender, or potato masher

- Gallon plastic freezer bag

- Measuring cups and spoons

- Medium baking dish or oven-safe skillet

- Mixing bowls: 2 small and 2 medium to large

- Storage containers
  » 21 (20- to 25-ounce) containers including:
    » 4 mason jars
    » 7 containers with 2 or 3 divided sections

- Whisk

Week 6

	Breakfast	Lunch	Dinner
Day 1	Spinach and Cheese Egg Muffins	Mediterranean Mason Jar Salad	Olive Chicken with Potatoes
Day 2	Peanut Butter Fruit Dip	Mediterranean Mason Jar Salad	Garlic Parmesan Pasta
Day 3	Spinach and Cheese Egg Muffins	Garlic Hummus Lunch Box	Olive Chicken with Potatoes
Day 4	Peanut Butter Fruit Dip	Mediterranean Mason Jar Salad	Garlic Parmesan Pasta
Day 5	Spinach and Cheese Egg Muffins	Garlic Hummus Lunch Box	Olive Chicken with Potatoes
Day 6	Peanut Butter Fruit Dip	Garlic Hummus Lunch Box	Garlic Parmesan Pasta
Day 7	Spinach and Cheese Egg Muffins	Garlic Hummus Lunch Box	Olive Chicken with Potatoes

Step-by-Step Meal Prep

1. Preheat the oven to 400°F. Make the Olive Chicken with Potatoes (page 114) through step 2.

2. While the potatoes bake and the chicken marinates, make the Mediterranean Mason Jar Salad (page 113) and the Peanut Butter Fruit Dip (page 111).

3. When the potatoes finish baking, reduce the heat and complete step 3 of the Olive Chicken with Potatoes recipe. Then complete the Spinach and Cheese Egg Muffins (page 110) through step 3.

4. While the egg muffins bake, make the Garlic Hummus Lunch Box (page 112).

5. Last, make the Garlic Parmesan Pasta (page 116) and finish the Spinach and Cheese Egg Muffins while the Olive Chicken with Potatoes finishes baking.

6. Portion, pack, label, and store! Freeze two portions of Olive Chicken with Potatoes, one portion of Garlic Parmesan Pasta, and one portion of Spinach and Cheese Egg Muffins.

Spinach and Cheese Egg Muffins

PREP TIME: 15 minutes | **COOK TIME:** 25 minutes | **SERVES** 4 (3 muffins each)
REFRIGERATOR: Up to 5 days | **FREEZER:** Up to 30 days

Eggs are a common breakfast item in a Mediterranean diet, and contrary to popular belief, they provide healthy fats and nutrients like vitamin A. Try these frittata-like "muffins" on a bed of leafy greens, or in a wrap with some black beans and salsa!

Nonstick cooking spray
12 large eggs
½ cup plain Greek yogurt
1 tablespoon minced garlic in olive oil
1 teaspoon freshly ground black pepper
4 cups spinach, chopped

1 medium jalapeño pepper, seeded and diced
½ red bell pepper, seeded and diced
½ medium red onion, diced
1 cup shredded cheddar cheese

1. Preheat the oven to 375°F. Spray a 12-muffin tin with nonstick cooking spray.
2. In a large bowl, whisk the eggs, yogurt, garlic, and black pepper until combined. Add the spinach, jalapeño, bell pepper, and onion, stirring to combine. Pour the mixture into the muffin tin and evenly sprinkle the cheese on top.
3. Bake for 18 to 22 minutes, until the tops of the muffins are golden brown and a toothpick inserted in the center comes out clean.
4. Let cool for 5 to 10 minutes before removing from the tin. Place 3 muffins each in 4 containers.

REHEAT: Heat in the microwave on high in 30-second increments until the center is hot. If frozen, thaw in the refrigerator before reheating.

Calories: 373; Total fat: 25g; Saturated fat: 11g; Sodium: 412mg; Carbohydrates: 8g; Fiber: 1g; Protein: 28g; Calcium: 352mg; Potassium: 542mg

Peanut Butter Fruit Dip

PREP TIME: 5 minutes | **COOK TIME:** 5 minutes | **SERVES** 3 (2 waffles each)
REFRIGERATOR: Up to 7 days | **FREEZER:** Up to 3 months

Jazz up your fruit with this simple dip. High-protein Greek yogurt is another common ingredient in Mediterranean diets and is more tart in taste than traditional yogurt. The yogurt and the peanut butter also provide protein to make your fruit more satisfying and keep you fuller for longer.

1½ cups plain Greek yogurt
½ cup no-salt-added creamy
    peanut butter
2 tablespoons honey

1 teaspoon vanilla extract
6 frozen whole-wheat waffles
3 cups seedless grapes

1. In a medium bowl, whisk the yogurt, peanut butter, honey, and vanilla until it is a smooth consistency.
2. Toast the waffles well and cut them into quarters.
3. Divide the dip equally into 3 containers with 1 cup of grapes and 2 of the waffles in each.

PREP TIP: Use a container with 3 divided sections to store the dip separately from the grapes and the waffles.

VARIATION: Try this dip with any fruit of your choice like apples, pears, or strawberries. Store sliced apples or pears in a couple tablespoons of lemon or pineapple juice to prevent browning.

Calories: 660; Total fat: 32g; Saturated fat: 7g; Sodium: 445mg; Carbohydrates: 80g; Fiber: 6g; Protein: 22g; Calcium: 379mg; Potassium: 988mg

Garlic Hummus Lunch Box

PREP TIME: 15 minutes | **SERVES** 4 | **REFRIGERATOR:** Up to 7 days
FREEZER: Hummus can be stored for up to 6 months; not recommended to freeze
vegetables and pretzels

Chickpeas are commonly found in different Mediterranean cuisines.
Hummus, made mostly of mashed chickpeas, is a staple that every
family has its own unique recipe for. It's great as an appetizer or as
the star of the meal with this lunch box.

1 (15-ounce) can no-salt-added
    chickpeas
2 tablespoons olive oil
2 tablespoons water, plus more
    as needed
1 tablespoon minced garlic in olive oil

1 teaspoon ground cumin
Juice of ½ lemon
1 cucumber, cut into ½-inch slices
1 pound baby carrots
½ red bell pepper, cut into thin strips
2 cups low-sodium pretzels

1. In a food processor or blender, combine the chickpeas, olive oil, water,
   garlic, cumin, and lemon juice. Pulse until creamy and add 1 to 2 extra
   tablespoons of water to thin out if needed.
2. Divide the hummus evenly among 4 containers.
3. Add a quarter of the cucumbers, carrots, bell pepper strips, and pretzels to each container.

PREP TIP: Use a container with at least 2 divided sections to keep the
hummus separate from the vegetables and pretzels so they stay crispy.

VARIATION: No food processor or blender? No problem! You can mash the
chickpeas with a potato masher and mix by hand, or if you want to save
even more time, you can purchase premade hummus. Aim for an option
with less than 300mg sodium in a 2-tablespoon serving.

Calories: 336; Total fat: 10g; Saturated fat: 1g; Sodium: 164mg;
Carbohydrates: 55g; Fiber: 9g; Protein: 10g; Calcium: 97mg;
Potassium: 735mg

Mediterranean Mason Jar Salad

PREP TIME: 10 minutes | **SERVES** 3 | **REFRIGERATOR:** Up to 4 days
FREEZER: Not recommended

LOW SODIUM

GLUTEN-FREE

VEGETARIAN

Mason jars are a great tool for preventing salad from getting soggy by layering the toppings with the dressing in the bottom and the leafy greens on top. Layers of flavors, acidity from the tomato, saltiness from the olives, bitterness from the onions, and creamy sweetness from the feta bring the Mediterranean to life in this grab-and-go salad.

3 tablespoons olive oil
1 tablespoon balsamic vinegar
2 teaspoons minced garlic in olive oil
1 teaspoon Dijon mustard
1 teaspoon honey
¼ teaspoon freshly ground black pepper

12 pitted kalamata olives, sliced
1 cucumber, chopped
½ red onion, chopped
2 Roma or plum tomatoes, chopped
2 ounces crumbled feta cheese
3 cups fresh baby spinach

1. In a small bowl, whisk the olive oil, vinegar, garlic, mustard, honey, and pepper. Divide the dressing evenly among 3 mason jars.
2. Layer in the cucumber, onion, tomatoes, and olives, dividing them evenly among the jars, and add ⅔ ounce—about 1¼ tablespoons—of feta to each jar. Top each with 1 cup of spinach.

PREP TIP: Pickled olives can be high in sodium, so be sure to read the nutrition labels and try to choose olives with the lowest amount of sodium possible.

VARIATION: You can make endless varieties of mason jar salads. Start with the dressing on the bottom; then layer crunchy vegetables and more delicate ingredients like beans, grains, cheese, or eggs, and add leafy vegetables last.

Calories: 236; Total fat: 20g; Saturated fat: 5g; Sodium: 487mg; Carbohydrates: 12g; Fiber: 3g; Protein: 5g; Calcium: 157mg; Potassium: 474mg

Olive Chicken with Potatoes

PREP TIME: 50 minutes | **COOK TIME:** 2 hours 15 minutes | **SERVES** 4
REFRIGERATOR: Up to 5 days | **FREEZER:** Up to 6 months

Olives are another staple of the Mediterranean diet. You may have noticed the abundance of olive oil used throughout this book. This recipe incorporates the sour saltiness of the olive into a delicious chicken dish.

2 tablespoons olive oil, divided
1 tablespoon red wine vinegar
1 tablespoon Dijon mustard
1 tablespoon minced garlic in olive oil
½ tablespoon chopped fresh rosemary
4 chicken thighs (about 1½ pounds)

½ cup pitted kalamata olives
8 red potatoes, diced
½ teaspoon Italian seasoning
¼ teaspoon freshly ground black pepper
¼ cup dry white wine, such as chardonnay

1. Preheat the oven to 400°F. Line a baking sheet with parchment paper.
2. In a gallon plastic freezer bag, combine 1 tablespoon of olive oil, the vinegar, mustard, garlic, and rosemary. Add the chicken thighs and olives and marinate for at least 30 minutes.
3. In a medium bowl, toss the potatoes with the remaining 1 tablespoon of olive oil, the Italian seasoning, and the pepper. Spread the potatoes on the baking sheet and bake for 30 to 45 minutes, stirring occasionally until the potatoes are tender. Remove the potatoes from the oven and divide them equally into 4 containers.
4. Once the potatoes finish baking, reduce the heat to 375°F. Transfer the chicken, olives, and marinade to a 2-quart baking dish or large oven-safe skillet. Add the white wine and bake for 90 minutes, until the chicken is cooked through and the top is golden brown.
5. Allow the chicken to cool for 10 to 15 minutes. Add 1 chicken thigh to each container with the potatoes. Divide the olives and remaining sauce evenly among the 4 containers.

REHEAT: Microwave at 50 percent power for 2 minutes and then continue to heat in 1-minute increments until the chicken is heated through. In the oven, bake covered at 350°F for 15 to 20 minutes.

VARIATION: Substitute boneless, skinless chicken breasts and reduce the baking time to 45 to 50 minutes.

Calories: 574; Total fat: 28g; Saturated fat: 6g; Sodium: 320mg; Carbohydrates: 56g; Fiber: 7g; Protein: 25g; Calcium: 64mg; Potassium: 1,797mg

Garlic Parmesan Pasta

PREP TIME: 10 minutes | **COOK TIME:** 30 minutes | **SERVES** 3
REFRIGERATOR: Up to 5 days | **FREEZER:** Up to 3 months

This dish highlights the simplicity of the Mediterranean diet by focusing on a few ingredients with complementary flavors. The garlic, olive oil, and red pepper flakes marry to make the perfect sauce for this pasta dinner.

½ pound whole-wheat pasta
1 pound green beans
2 tablespoons olive oil
2 tablespoons minced garlic in olive oil

1 teaspoon red pepper flakes
¼ teaspoon freshly ground black pepper
¼ cup grated Parmesan cheese

1. Place a large saucepan three-quarters full of water over high heat and bring to a boil. Add the pasta and cook according to the package directions to al dente. Drain and set aside.
2. Steam the green beans. If they are in a steam bag, cook them in the microwave according to the package directions, then drain excess liquid. Or use a vegetable steamer in a medium saucepan on the stove. Fill the saucepan with water until it is just under the bottom of the steamer. Add the beans, cover, and bring to a boil. Keep covered and reduce the heat to medium-low. Steam for 5 minutes.
3. Heat the olive oil in a large skillet over medium heat and sauté the garlic, red pepper flakes, and black pepper for 2 to 3 minutes.
4. Add the green beans and pasta and toss in the sauce. Separate the pasta into 3 containers and top each with Parmesan cheese.

REHEAT: Add 1 teaspoon of water to the dish and partially cover it. Microwave in 30-second increments, stirring in between.

Calories: 433; Total fat: 13g; Saturated fat: 3g; Sodium: 167mg; Carbohydrates: 70g; Fiber: 11g; Protein: 17g; Calcium: 168mg; Potassium: 519mg

SODIUM-FREE FLAVORING GUIDE

	Beef	Pork	Poultry	Fish	Eggs	Vegetables
Citrus and Other Acidic Fruit	grape, grapefruit	apple, orange	cranberry, orange, pineapple	lemon, lime, orange	lemon, lime	lemon, lime, orange
Vinegars	balsamic, red wine	apple cider, white wine	apple cider, red wine, white wine	balsamic, malt, white wine	distilled white	balsamic, red wine, rice, white wine
Spices	caraway, curry, dry mustard, garlic, pepper	caraway, cloves, garlic, ginger, pepper	cloves, garlic, nutmeg, paprika, saffron, turmeric	curry, dry mustard, paprika, pepper, turmeric	curry, dry mustard, garlic, nutmeg, paprika, turmeric	cumin, garlic, ginger, nutmeg, pepper
Herbs	basil, bay leaf, dill, rosemary, sage	basil, chives, rosemary, thyme	basil, oregano, parsley, sage, thyme	basil, bay leaf, dill, tarragon	dill, parsley, rosemary, tarragon	basil, dill, rosemary, tarragon

MEASUREMENT CONVERSIONS

	us standard	us standard (ounces)	Metric (approximate)
VOLUME EQUIVALENTS (LIQUID)	2 tablespoons	1 fl. oz.	30 mL
	¼ cup	2 fl. oz.	60 mL
	½ cup	4 fl. oz.	120 mL
	1 cup	8 fl. oz.	240 mL
	1½ cups	12 fl. oz.	355 mL
	2 cups or 1 pint	16 fl. oz.	475 mL
	4 cups or 1 quart	32 fl. oz.	1 L
	1 gallon	128 fl. oz.	4 L
VOLUME EQUIVALENTS (DRY)	⅛ teaspoon		0.5 mL
	¼ teaspoon		1 mL
	½ teaspoon		2 mL
	¾ teaspoon		4 mL
	1 teaspoon		5 mL
	1 tablespoon		15 mL
	¼ cup		59 mL
	⅓ cup		79 mL
	½ cup		118 mL
	⅔ cup		156 mL
	¾ cup		177 mL
	1 cup		235 mL
	2 cups or 1 pint		475 mL
	3 cups		700 mL
	4 cups or 1 quart		1 L
	½ gallon		2 L
	1 gallon		4 L
WEIGHT EQUIVALENTS	½ ounce		15 g
	1 ounce		30 g
	2 ounces		60 g
	4 ounces		115 g
	8 ounces		225 g
	12 ounces		340 g
	16 ounces or 1 pound		455 g

	Fahrenheit (F)	celsius (C) (approximate)
OVEN TEMPERATURES	250°F	120°C
	300°F	150°C
	325°F	180°C
	375°F	190°C
	400°F	200°C
	425°F	220°C
	450°F	230°C

REFERENCES

"9 Out of 10 Americans Eat Too Much Sodium Infographic." Heart.org. Accessed August 4, 2021. heart.org/en/healthy-living/healthy-eating/eat-smart/sodium /9-out-of-10-americans-eat-too-much-sodium-infographic.

Abdelhamid, A. S., et al. "Polyunsaturated Fatty Acids for the Primary and Secondary Prevention of Cardiovascular Disease." *Cochrane Database of Systematic Reviews* 11 (2018). doi.org/10.1002/14651858.CD012345.pub3.

Bondonno, Nicola P., et al. "Associations between Fruit Intake and Risk of Diabetes in the AusDiab Cohort." *The Journal of Clinical Endocrinology & Metabolism* 106, no. 10 (October 2021). doi.org/10.1210/clinem/dgab335.

"Causes of Chronic Kidney Disease | NIDDK." National Institute of Diabetes and Digestive and Kidney Diseases. Accessed June 19, 2021. niddk.nih.gov/health -information/kidney-disease/chronic-kidney-disease-ckd/causes.

Center for Food Safety and Applied Nutrition. "Food Labeling & Nutrition." FDA. June 9, 2021. fda.gov/food/food-labeling-nutrition.

Centers for Disease Control and Prevention. "The Role of Sodium in Your Food." September 8, 2020. cdc.gov/salt/role_of_sodium.htm.

Dernini, S., et al. "Med Diet 4.0: The Mediterranean Diet with Four Sustainable Benefits." *Public Health Nutrition* 20, no. 7 (May 2017): 1322–30. *PubMed*. doi.org/10.1017 /S1368980016003177.

Galbete, Cecilia, et al. "Nordic Diet, Mediterranean Diet, and the Risk of Chronic Diseases: The EPIC-Potsdam Study." *BMC Medicine* 16, no. 1 (2018): 99. doi.org/10.1186/s12916-018-1082-y.

Hatfield, Heather. "Mixing Plastic and Food: An Urban Legend?" *WebMD*. Accessed June 29, 2021. webmd.com/food-recipes/features/mixing-plastic-food -urban-legend.

Juraschek, Stephen P., et al. "Effects of Sodium Reduction and the DASH Diet in Relation to Baseline Blood Pressure." *Journal of the American College of Cardiology* 70, no. 23 (December 2017): 2841–48. doi.org/10.1016/j.jacc.2017.10.011.

McRae, Marc P. "Dietary Fiber Is Beneficial for the Prevention of Cardiovascular Disease: An Umbrella Review of Meta-Analyses." *Journal of Chiropractic Medicine* 16, no. 4 (December 2017): 289–99. doi.org/10.1016/j.jcm.2017.05.005.

Office of the Commissioner. "Federal Food, Drug, and Cosmetic Act (FD&C Act)." FDA. Last modified March 29, 2018. fda.gov/regulatory-information/laws-enforced-fda/federal-food-drug-and-cosmetic-act-fdc-act.

"Quiznos Sub Sandwich Restaurants—Nutrition Info." *Quiznos.* Accessed June 24, 2021. quiznos.com/wp-content/uploads/2021/10/Quiznos_Nutritionals_U.S_101421.pdf

Salas-Salvadó, Jordi, et al. "Protective Effects of the Mediterranean Diet on Type 2 Diabetes and Metabolic Syndrome." *The Journal of Nutrition* 146, no. 4 (April 2016): 920S–72S. doi.org/10.3945/jn.115.218487.

Yao, Baodong, et al. "Dietary Fiber Intake and Risk of Type 2 Diabetes: A Dose–Response Analysis of Prospective Studies." *European Journal of Epidemiology* 29, no. 2 (February 2014): 79–88. doi.org/10.1007/s10654-013-9876-x.

INDEX

About the Author

AYLA SHAW, RDN, MS, is a board-certified registered dietitian nutritionist in private practice on St. Thomas in the Virgin Islands. She obtained her master's degree in nutrition at Georgia State University before traveling to Connecticut to complete her dietetic internship focused in clinical nutrition at Yale New Haven Hospital.

Upon finishing her internship, Ayla followed her heart (aka a boy) and moved to the Virgin Islands. She was living on St. Thomas and employed by Schneider Regional Medical Center when Hurricane Irma hit on September 6, 2017.

Ayla began her personal blog and website in the wake of the storms to provide a resource for nutrition information focused on combating the epidemic of chronic disease on St. Thomas. Today, she owns and operates Island RDN, a nutrition consulting company that offers outpatient counseling through several locations on St. Thomas. Additionally, Ayla works as a consultant and freelance food and health writer. When she is not working, she enjoys spending time at the beach with her family and her dog, Dobby.

Follow Ayla online at IslandRDN.com or @islandRDN.